STEPHANIE DIANI

PENGUIN BOOKS

GRAMMAR SNOBS ARE GREAT BIG MEANIES

June Casagrande is a writer and journalist whose weekly column, "A Word, Please," appears in several community news supplements to the *Los Angeles Times*. She has written articles for a number of regional and national publications, and has worked as an editor and copy editor. Casagrande was born in New York City, grew up in the Clearwater / St. Petersburg / Tampa area, and now lives in Pasadena, California.

For more information, visit www.grammarsnobs.com

GRAMMAR SNOBS
Are
Great Big
MEANIES

*A Guide to Language
for Fun and Spite*

June Casagrande

Penguin Books

PENGUIN BOOKS

Published by the Penguin Group

Penguin Group (USA) Inc., 375 Hudson Street, New York,
New York 10014, U.S.A.
Penguin Group (Canada), 90 Eglinton Avenue East, Suite 700, Toronto,
Ontario, Canada M4P 2Y3 (a division of Pearson Penguin Canada Inc.)
Penguin Books Ltd, 80 Strand, London WC2R 0RL, England
Penguin Ireland, 25 St Stephen's Green, Dublin 2, Ireland
(a division of Penguin Books Ltd)
Penguin Group (Australia), 250 Camberwell Road, Camberwell, Victoria 3124,
Australia (a division of Pearson Australia Group Pty Ltd)
Penguin Books India Pvt Ltd, 11 Community Centre,
Panchsheel Park, New Delhi – 110 017, India
Penguin Group (NZ), cnr Airborne and Rosedale Roads, Albany, Auckland
1310, New Zealand (a division of Pearson New Zealand Ltd)
Penguin Books (South Africa) (Pty) Ltd, 24 Sturdee Avenue, Rosebank,
Johannesburg 2196, South Africa

Penguin Books Ltd, Registered Offices:
80 Strand, London WC2R 0RL, England

First published in Penguin Books 2006

5   7   9   10   8   6

Copyright © June Casagrande, 2006
All rights reserved

LIBRARY OF CONGRESS CATALOGING IN PUBLICATION DATA
Casagrande, June.
Grammar snobs are great big meanies : a guide to language for fun and spite / by
June Casagrande.
p. cm.
Includes bibliographical references.
ISBN 0 14 30.3683 1
1. English language—Usage.   2. English language—Usage—Humor.   I. Title.
PE1460.C325 2006
428'.02'07—dc22   2005053179

Printed in the United States of America
Set in Janson Text and Journal Text
Designed by Sabrina Bowers

For Ted

A Note from the Author

I'd like to thank Bryan Garner, Robert Hartwell Fiske, James Kilpatrick, Richard Lederer, Laurie Rozakis, Lynne Truss, William Safire, Bill Walsh, all the readers of my column who earned mention here, and all the editors of the *Associated Press Stylebook*, the *Chicago Manual of Style*, and the *Oxford English Grammar* for being such great sports. Like, wow, do these people have an awesome sense of humor or what? Well, actually I'm writing my thank-yous before any of them have even had a chance to read this book. But I just know that I'm not going to catch any of them hiding in the bushes outside my house with a carton of rotten eggs, or worse.

So let's hear it for the people who, as I poke fun at them, just laugh in the spirit in which the jabs were written—the people who never lose sight of the fact that we're all on the same team of helping others better use the language. **You guys rock!**

Contents

Grammar Snobs Make Good Prison Brides

Dear June,

It seems that you do not agree that only adverbs can modify verbs (hence the name "adverb"), because you are making the same mistake in your recent article. In the sentence ". . . makes you sound like a snob at best or, if you use it wrong, like a fool at worst." One cannot use anything "wrong," only "wrongly." "Incorrectly" would be a more appropriate adverb to use.

I have noticed that the rare times you include readers' comments on mistakes made in your articles are when there may be differences in opinion on correct usage. In your incorrect use of "wrong," there is no doubt that you are wrong.

I therefor challenge you to admit your mistake in a follow-up article for all to read. I am not holding my breath.

Signed,
Mario

Dear June:

English Grammar. Chapter 1. Nouns, Adjectives and Adverbs. Consider your sentence: ". . . makes you sound like a snob at best or, if you use it wrong, like a fool at worst." "Wrong" can be used as a noun or an adjective, but never an adverb. For example: June was wrong. "Wrong" is a noun, the object of the verb "was."

June used the wrong word. Wrong is an adjective describing the noun "word." June used the word wrongly. Wrongly is an adverb modifying the verb used. I look forward to reading your "mea culpa" in your next article.

Signed,

spgs19401947 via e-mail

Dear Mario and Spgs:

Please open your dictionaries to the word "wrong." Please see that, following the first cluster of definitions under "adj.," adjective, comes the abbreviation "adv." Adverb. "Wrong" is an adverb. And you are both wrong.

—June

As I've learned since I began writing a weekly grammar column in a community news supplement to the *Los Angeles Times* called the *Daily Pilot*, no one knows "enough" about grammar. This causes a lot of people to feel insecure and alone, as if they're the only ones whose grasp of the language is less than adequate. But for the rare and vicious breed that is the grammar snob, other people's insecurities are an opportunity to humiliate. The snobs don't know "enough" about grammar, either—many of the issues that perplex their victims baffle these self-appointed experts as well. But they use their random bits of knowledge to bluff and bludgeon their way to an unwarranted sense of superiority.

For someone who's been victimized by a grammar snob, it's easy to lump all word aficionados into the same category. But we should be careful here. We must be fair. Grammar snobs are a distinct breed from their gentle cousins: word nerds and grammar geeks. The difference is bloodlust.

Word nerds and grammar geeks might find it fascinating to know that the word "gerrymander" comes from nineteenth-century Massachusetts governor Elbridge Gerry (bless their little hearts), or they might actually try to quote Shakespeare to their auto mechanics, but they're a separate species from the types who send me raging e-mails about how no one uses the word "whom" anymore or the ones who write to me demanding I publish a column telling people to stop using profanity (*!#@$! weirdos).

Since I started writing my column, these meanies treat me like the guy in the bar everyone else wants to beat the stuffing out of because he's reputedly a good fighter. That's certainly not the role I wanted. In fact, I bang the humility drum so hard that I think I might qualify for admission to a monastery. And Mario and Spgs are perfect examples of why I'm so big on the whole humility thing: In grammar and language, if you go around picking fights, it's just a matter of time before you find yourself facedown on the barroom floor with boot prints all over your back.

Yet the bullies keep on trying to bully us.

No more.

It's time, oh yes, it's time for the rest of us to stand up to these snobs—to call their bluff. If not for our own edification, if not to gain a better command of the language and all the doors it opens for us—at the very least we must learn a little about grammar and usage for the sheer thrill of taking down these grammar tyrants, one at a time, just to watch them fall.

For example, the two people who "wrongly" reamed me got their wish: a public airing of the issue in the September 27, 2004, *Daily Pilot*. As I pointed out in this flogging, "wrong" and "right" are both adjectives and adverbs. You can say, "Mario is wrong," which is an adjective, like "Mario is angry." Or you can say, "Mario used the word wrong," which is an adverb because it modifies the verb "used." In case you're a little rusty, adverbs mainly modify verbs, whereas adjectives modify things, people, and places.

And, unless you're in the presence of Mario or Spgs, you can use the word "right" without fear as well. You don't need to say, "I did it rightly." Your first instinct, "I did it right," is right.

Now, for anyone who's been itching to point out other mistakes in Mario's and Spgs's e-mails, let me caution you to use humility. For example, some of you may have noticed the word "therefor" in Mario's e-mail and subsequently felt an inflated sense of self-esteem, an intoxicating rush of superiority. Beware. Like all intoxicants, this one has a way of leaving you dazed and humiliated.

You see, "therefor" is, in fact, a word. But unfortunately for Mario, he used it wrong. "Therefor," which is most often seen in legal writing, is not considered part of modern English. It's archaic and means "for that." The more commonly used "therefore," meaning "hence" or "for this reason," is the one he should have used.

Spgs was wrong when she or he said that "wrong" is a noun in the sentence "June was wrong." It's not a noun; it's an adjective. It's like "Spgs is tall," "Spgs is unhappy," or "Spgs is confused."

"Wrong" can be a noun, just not the way Spgs explained. Think of "to commit a wrong." That's a noun.

So why would someone who didn't bother opening a dictionary fire off such harsh and oh-so-certain e-mails? Sure, one could be a fluke. But two? In the same week? Could that be a fluke?

Nope. It's a recurring phenomenon.

For example, years ago, a reporter at the newspaper where I worked typed the word "peaked" when she meant to write "piqued," as in, "Something piqued my curiosity." The editors didn't catch the mistake and it showed up in the paper. A few days later, the reporter received in the mail a clipping of her article with the mistake circled next to a single handwritten word: "Idiot!"

Then there was the guy who mailed to me a photocopy of a letter that he had been fiendishly clutching for more than a decade.

July 18, 1991

Dear Mr. (Name Omitted)

Thanks for the letter about the grammatical errors in the article about women in combat. You are right, of course, and we deserve to be embarrassed. Such errors are usually a result of haste, not ignorance, but that does not excuse them.

I hope we won't soon give you a similar reason to write again.

Best regards,
William Borders
Senior Editor,
New York Times

Ironically, attached to the photocopied letter was a typewritten Post-it note that read, "This is now a real journalist deals with 'scary' letters." (No, that's not a typo. He wrote, "This is *now*," instead of "This is *how*." Fun, I know. But I suspect the irony would be wasted on a guy who saves letters like this and who puts tiny little Post-it pages into a typewriter.)

Then there was the time, years before, when I wrote a feature story about a farrier—a person who shoes horses for a living. One of the little subheadlines in the article was, "A Shoe-In."

Had someone sent me a note to criticize what a groaningly bad pun that was, I'd have not only accepted the criticism, I would have agreed with it. But apparently, the giddy rush a grammar snob experiences upon encountering a potential language error eclipses everything akin to a sense of humor. I received in the mail something called a "No-No Card" from a local language society telling me that I meant to write, "A Shoo-In."

Had the sender of this "No-No Card" included a return address, I'd have told her exactly what I'd like to put my shoe in.

So what is it that makes these people so very, very mean? Well, I'm not sure, really. But it's all too clear that a little bit of grammar knowledge in the wrong hands is a dangerous thing, kind of like the One Ring in the hands of anybody but Frodo.

As you'll see in the pages that follow, most of the fear they breed and spread is completely unfounded. Even the snobs who actually know their stuff are nothing to fear, because half the time when they cite a language "rule" they're neglecting to mention that these things are just judgment calls that you are as qualified to make as they are—issues about which experts disagree and sometimes even confess to being stumped.

So if you ever find yourself being roughed up by people

who actually expect you to say ridiculously stuffy-sounding things like, "I did it wrongly," or "I followed the directions rightly," just know that, eventually, all grammar bullies get their comeuppance. Even better, with a little confidence you can be the one who puts them in their place.

Okay, maybe spite isn't the best reason to learn grammar and usage. And maybe it isn't a basis for life. And maybe it doesn't justify the things I wrote about William Safire on the bathroom wall of the HotStudz nightclub in West Hollywood. But it's certainly good motivation. What's more, the meanies—just by being themselves—have provided us with excellent fodder for having a good time while we learn. In the following chapters, we'll give these snobs the figurative de-pantsing they deserve and even some bashing so rough that they probably don't deserve it. I'm okay with that.

I'm pretty sure our ends justify our means, because, as we'll see, the rules of language function like one big conspiracy to make most of us feel stupid. And because, as we're already beginning to see, grammar snobs really are great big meanies.

GRAMMAR
SNOBS
Are
Great Big
MEANIES

Chapter 1

A Snob for All Seasons

Shared Possessives

Grammar snobs come in two forms: amateur and pro. Amateur grammar snobs are a lot like amateur gynecologists—they're everywhere, they're all too eager to offer their services, and they're anything but gentle. They include the guy at the party who says, "From where did you get the recipe for this torte?" and the girl who likes to point out your dangler and laugh, and the old biddy who was beside herself with malicious glee the time I accidentally wrote "old bitty."

These people are scary enough, but what's worse is that there also exists a whole crop of cranks who actually make a living at being meanies.

Meet James Kilpatrick, syndicated columnist and grammar grouch extraordinaire. Kilpatrick is a guy who actually writes stuff like, "It is time, once again, for propounding a paean to the period. Heavenly dot! Divine orb! Precious pea of punctuation! Let us pray for their unceasing employment!"

I shtick you not. This was the opening paragraph of Kilpatrick's November 1, 2004, "The Writer's Art" column.

In Kilpatrick's defense I should say: He's half kidding. In my defense I should say: He's half serious. Sure, he's using over-the-top, punctuation-drunk terms to exaggerate his love for the period, but I can assure you that he didn't just pull this stuff out of his Underwood. No, this linguo-erotic rant bubbled up from some dark place deep within, carrying with it a large red flag alerting normal people to the state of this guy's inky soul.

In his flowery spiel, Kilpatrick displays one of the most classic signs of grammar snobbery and an important thing for the rest of us to note. You see, as much as we tend to think of language snobs as frothy-mouthed meanies who spew bitterness day and night, in reality the meanies aren't cranky all the time. Sometimes they can be downright chipper.

That's when they're really scary.

Unlike normal people who get giddy about things like love, sex, money, free beer, and classic REO Speedwagon, these guys have the hots for things like punctuation marks and syntax rules and the excavation of lost words that were lost for a reason.

Like a lot of "happy" drunks, these people can turn on you in an instant, transforming from Jekyll-like, playful nerds into bloodthirsty grammar Hydes. Think I'm exaggerating? Then compare the above Kilpatrick excerpt to what immediately followed.

"Why this unseemly ruckus?" Kilpatrick continued. "I shall explain—regretfully explain. On October 4, *The New Yorker* magazine carried 1,500 words of truly abominable editing. The piece was a think-piece of little thought. It started nowhere, went nowhere and arrived at no interesting destination."

As the *Seinfeld* characters put it when they tried to imitate a vicious catfight: "Reer!"

His venom was just to make the point that very long sentences are bad and that periods can make them shorter. I suppose that, in the interest of filling up blank paper, Kilpatrick had to milk the idea for all the words he could get, but in the process, you can't deny that he brings a whole new meaning to the term "to be on one's period."

William Safire, author of the "On Language" column in the *New York Times Magazine*, does a better job of keeping bipolarity in check. But upon closer inspection, it's clear that he has quite a bit in common with his colleagues.

In his December 12, 2004, column Safire describes himself as an "excruciating curmudgeon" and then goes on to demonstrate. In the same column, he high-fives author and fellow language meanie Robert Hartwell Fiske by proudly describing Fiske's and his own readers like this: "Our audience is composed of (not comprised of) people who get a delicious kick out of getting incensed at loosey-goosey language."

Yuck.

In a 1980 piece, Safire demonstrates a surprising capacity for understanding the dangers of language superiority. "Some of the interest in the world of words comes from people who like to put less-educated people down—Language Snobs, who give good usage a bad name." But after authoring that piece, Safire went on to spend the next twenty-five years writing columns that snootily drop more names than you can count. In a single "On Language" column reprinted in his book *Coming to Terms*, Safire makes reference to Hermes, Mercury, Library of Congress manuscript division chief James H. Hutson, Warren Harding, Roger Sherman, Max Farrand, Attorney General Edwin L. Meese III, seventeenth-century theological author Richard Burthogge, editor Hugh J. Silverman, Zeus, Martin Heidegger, Irving Kristol, Jacques Derrida, Shakespeare, Coleridge, Stuart Berg Flexner, and Heritage Foundation constitutional specialist Bruce Fein.

So much for our great defender of the less-educated little guy.

Perhaps it's no coincidence that both Kilpatrick and Safire have had long careers as political columnists—conservative political columnists. And perhaps the fact that one William F. Buckley Jr. authored one of the language books at my local library is further evidence of something funny going on here. It's certainly not my place to speculate whether there exists any correlation between conservative political punditry and up-tight, anal, quasi-erotic obsession with impossibly strict language rules and/or mean-spirited superiority. My job here is only to examine the shared affliction of these men to consider the question: What crawled up their behinds and died?

For argument's sake, let's say it was a bug.

So, transitioning not so gracefully into the lesson phase of this chapter, would you say, "A bug crawled up Kilpatrick's and Safire's behinds and died"? Or would you omit the first apostrophe and "s" and instead say, "It crawled up Kilpatrick and Safire's behinds"?

Though both sentences have a certain on-the-money ring to them, the first one sounds better, doesn't it? That's because the question of whether to use the extra apostrophe and "s" has to do with whether the possession is shared or separate.

If Kilpatrick and Safire shared two behinds, you would say, "Safire and Kilpatrick's butts." If they shared a single behind, it would be "Safire and Kilpatrick's butt. (And no doubt it would also have to work double overtime to expel both men's special brand of genius.)

But because it's safe to assume that each man has his own distinct and vise-tight posterior, you would say, "Safire's and Kilpatrick's butts."

No doubt right now you're probably thinking, "This whole question is ridiculous. A single bug could not have crawled up both their butts and died, unless of course it was some kind of super zombie bug that can rise from the dead to irritate again."

So, looking forward to the day when science can transcend such limitations and genetically engineer a fanny-loving phoenix bug, I concede that, for now, you're right.

Chapter 2

For Whom the Snob Trolls

"Who"/"Whom" and Why You're Right Not to Care

You can hate the word "whom," but you've got to love what a good tool it is for knowing when you're dealing with a grammar snob. What normal person stands in the middle of the sales office at work and says, "So Joe, you're taking whom to the Slayer concert on Friday?" or "Guess with whom I have a date Saturday night"?

People who talk like this, you and I well know, can't get a date at all. Ever. Most of them must make do with fuzzy memories of a middle school English teacher or with a surreptitiously acquired snapshot of the local librarian.

People who talk like this also have done an incredible job of alienating the rest of us from even wanting to know how to use the word "whom." In fact, we've gotten to a point where most language authorities say "whom" is required only in formal speech and writing. But there's a good reason to learn. So good that it's worth overcoming the visceral aversion to the word that these grammar snobs have instilled in us. And here is that reason: About half the people you hear spewing the word "whom" in everyday conversation don't really know how.

They're bluffing. They know just enough to get it right sometimes—that's all they need to make themselves feel like big shots. And they're gambling you're not equipped to bust them cold.

And here's another reason, one you won't believe until you see it with your own eyes: You already know how to use the word "whom." You just don't know you know.

Consider this: When was the last time you said, "Me go to store now," or "Britney Spears? I love she!" or "Us are coming over for dinner"? I mean, not counting that time you were hypnotized into believing you were a caveman.

If you're a native English speaker, you already have an innate understanding of what we'll call "subject pronouns" and "object pronouns." (Most of the grammar books use the terms "nominative" and "subjective," respectively, to describe this difference. But my way's easier.) While it's normal to just glaze over when you hear these terms, if you stop and take notice, you'll see that they're completely self-explanatory.

Subject pronouns are the subjects of sentences. Object pronouns are the objects. In "I humiliated the grammar snob," "I" is the subject, "humiliated" is the verb or action, and "grammar snob" is the object—the thing the verb is acting upon. Which is why, if you shortened that, you'd say, "I humiliated him," not "I humiliated he."

So, the who/whom puzzle isn't a puzzle at all. "Who" is a subject, just as "I," "he," "she," "they," and "we" are subjects. "Whom" is an object, just like "me," "him," "her," "them," and "us." (Try not to think about "you" and "it." Their subject and object forms are the same.)

But it gets better. You can take a pen and scratch out everything I wrote above, then bonk yourself over the head with this book until you forget what you just read and *still* get it right almost every time. Here's how: Whenever you're wondering whether some blowhard is using "who" or "whom" right, plug in just about any other pronoun: I/me, she/her, he/him, we/us.

For, "With whom are you going to the concert?" ask yourself, would you say, "With he," or "With him"? For "Who is the best grammar-snob slayer of them all?" ask yourself if it would be better to say, "Him is the best grammar-snob slayer of them all," or "He is the best grammar-snob slayer."

It's just that simple.

Of course, it gets a little trickier when it's in a sentence with more than one verb, like, "I'll go to the concert with whoever loves heavy metal enough to pay me three hundred dollars for my extra ticket." That's because the "whoever" is an object of one action—"I'll go to the concert with"—but "whoever" is also performing another action: loving heavy metal music. So the rule is when it's both an object and a subject, the subject form always wins.

Don't let this scare you. That's what the grammar snobs want. And if we retreat now, the meanies win. Just remember this simple and very not-scary rule: Anytime the person being referred to is performing any action at all (that is, is the subject of any verb at all), don't use the letter "m." "Who loves heavy metal music," not "Whom loves heavy metal music."

The only truly scary thing about "whom" is a rule so arcane and obscure that pretty much nobody on the planet knows it anyway. And if you ever really feel like messing with a meanie's head, there's nothing better.

First, ask your grammar snob to explain how to use "whom." No doubt, he'll give the same basic spiel on object pronouns. Then say to your snob, "Okay. So according to your explanation, whenever someone knocks at your door you should yell, 'Whom is it' instead of 'Who is it,' right?"

If your grammar snob is smart, he'll burst into tears and run out of the room straight to his "happy place" in the library parking lot, near the window where the librarian sits. But chances are he's not that smart and he'll scramble to explain the situation. And, unless he's actually better versed at grammar than language book author William F. Buckley Jr., he'll fail.

The trickiest use of "who" versus "whom" is so esoteric that countless professional wordsmiths, including Buckley, have been busted getting it wrong. The answer lies in something called the "predicate nominative," which is the same reason you say on the phone, "This is he" instead of "This is him." (This topic is covered at length and quite sexily in chapter 30.) The rule is that a pronoun that follows some form of "to be" always takes the form of a subject. "This is she." "It is I." "The Slayer fan is he." Of course, this isn't how most of us really talk, but this is the rule that comes into play in these who/whom choices.

When you take a sentence such as, "Never mind whom I saw," and throw in an "it is," that little "is" is creating a predicate nominative, making it correct to say, "Never mind who it is I saw." That's also why you say, "Who is it?" and not "Whom is it?" Because, according to the predicate nominative, the answer is, "It is he," not "It is him." And that's something that will shut up both your Slayer fan and Buckley himself.

And while "whom" is arguably one for the scrap heap, there's another instance in which knowing the difference between subject and object pronouns is actually very useful.

How many times have you heard otherwise language-savvy people say things like, "John and I," when they mean "John and me"? The brightest people I know, and even newspaper editors, fall prey to saying and writing things like, "I'm so glad you could celebrate this occasion with Lisa and I," or "If you have any questions come talk to Steve or I," or "Just between you and I."

Just as we saw with "whom," to know when to use "John and I" versus "John and me" there's no need to ponder object pronouns. Just try dropping dear John, or Lisa, or Steve. That is, try the sentence just "I" or "me." "I'm so glad you could celebrate this occasion with I"? Or "with me"? "Come talk to I," or "Come talk to me"?

So, "Whom's afraid of the big bad grammar snob?" or "Who's afraid of the big bad grammar snob?" Not you, that's for sure.

Chapter 3

Passing the
Simpsons Test

It's "Till," Not "'Til"

In an episode of *The Simpsons*, mother Marge says she wishes she were going to the grammar rodeo. Then she pauses and wonders aloud, "Or is it, I wish I *was* going to the grammar rodeo?" Turns out there was no need to second-guess herself. She'd gotten it right the first time.

In another episode, the Simpsons find themselves mixed up with a motorcycle gang, the Hell's Satans. When Marge pronounces the word "résumé" by putting the stress on the last vowel, a biker named Ramrod politely questions her choice. "I believe it's pronounced 'RÉ-su-mé.'" The leader of this drunken and violent gang, played by John Goodman, intervenes: "Actually, both are acceptable."

Then there's the very old episode in which aspiring scout Bart is studying knife safety. The book he reads discusses "The Do's and Don'ts" of safely using knives—an expression that the writers or the animators or someone managed to punctuate well.

When the Springfield Elementary school bus washes up on a deserted island, Bart says, in surprisingly correct verb conjugation, "We should have just swum for it."

When the Simpsons attend a WNBA game, Bart hollers to basketball pro Lisa Leslie, "You got game." Leslie's reply: "You mean I *have* game." Bart then cheers, "You go, girl!" Leslie replies, "Yes, I will depart, lest your bad grammar rub off on me."

These impressive examples of language wisdom were uncovered as part of a highly scientific survey of broadcast television programming in which I set out to identify the most grammatically and linguistically superior show on television. My research went as follows: I watched hours and hours of *Simpsons* episodes, sometimes three reruns a day. I did this for the better part of a decade. I watched and rewatched reruns I'd rewatched before. I watched new episodes while also recording them so that I could watch them again the next day. I watched so many *Simpsons* episodes that I could recite some lines before they were spoken. I watched so many that I lost the ability to relate to three-dimensional beings. I watched these *Simpsons* episodes—and not much else.

At the end of this thorough and scientific survey period, I deduced conclusively that *The Simpsons* is indeed the most grammatically and linguistically savvy show on television. (I had suspected as much.) Where else can you hear an eight-year-old use words like "perspicacity" and "phallocentric"? Where else can you hear anyone use the word "crapulence"? What other cartoon has written scripts that include definitions for "abattoir" (slaughterhouse), "voluptuary" (a sensualist), and "satiety" (the state of being sated)?

The *Simpsons* writers got it right when they wrote "Ladies' Night" on a sign at the Quimby compound. They got it right when Patty said of her deceased aunt Gladys, "She was a role model for Selma and me." They scored when, in a recent episode, Lisa explained to Homer the difference between "imply" and "infer." And the show received the ultimate linguistic honor when Homer's trademark exclamation, "D'oh!" won a spot in the *Oxford English Dictionary*—despite the fact that the show's writers denote this sound in their scripts not with the word "d'oh" but with the term "annoyed grunt."

Clearly, *The Simpsons* is a shining beacon of prime-time language enlightenment.

But there's one thing they consistently get wrong. Every time I've seen them shorten the word "until," such as in signs on stores or in Moe's Bar, they write " 'til." "Drink 'til you barf." "Laugh 'til you care." "Plop 'til you drop." Stuff like that. Looks good, makes sense, seems logical, but just happens to be wrong. The shortened alternative to "until" is "till."

I'll pause while you check your dictionary. I understand why you might not want to just take my word for it. After all, what language gods in their right minds would shorten a word by throwing on an extra letter at the end, as if the original word had been "untill" all along? Ijits, I suppose, or evil folk. People who either don't get or despise the simplicity of shortening words by subtracting letters and adding the occasional apostrophe. People who know we're all accustomed to the simple and elegant logic in the well-known phrase, " 'Tis the season to be jolly," and who therein saw an opportunity to trip us up. People who couldn't stand to leave common sense on autopilot. People who have less language sense than the makers of a cartoon show.

Writing " 'til" instead of "till" is a mistake I myself made for a very long time. But for this one, I feel no shame, no urge to yell, "D'oh!" After all, the entire time I was getting it wrong, I was in very good company.

Chapter 4

To Boldly Blow

Only Windbags Fuss over Split Infinitives

The original *Star Trek* series bestowed many precious gifts on the world: fashions for half-naked alien women who want to look their best in death matches with starship captains; a wide-spread fear of sparkly gaseous masses; a deep and profound understanding that power-drunk tyrants are really just lonely little boys; the progressive political concept that rocks have feelings too; and endless possible punch lines that are variations on, "Dammit, Jim! I'm a doctor, not a _____!"

But along with these priceless cultural gems, *Star Trek* also gave us our most famous example of a split infinitive. Don't stop me if you've heard this one before: "These are the voyages of the starship *Enterprise*. Its five-year mission to explore strange new worlds, to seek out new life and new civilizations, to boldly go where no man has gone before."

As much as certain types love escaping into a fantasy world in which their knowledge of the Klingon language is a social asset and not a liability, meanies love to pounce on this famous opening line as evidence of their linguistic superiority.

In case you've been lucky enough to dodge the lecture, here's the concept. It's a simple one.

An infinitive is basically the main form of any verb, and in

English it includes the word "to." "To explore," "to trek," "to beam up"—these are all verbs in the infinitive form. To put them to use in different situations, you conjugate them. You conjugate "to walk" as "I walk, he walks, we walk," etcetera.

But to understand this "to boldly go" stuff, all you need to know is that the "to" is part of the whole. "To go" is a single unit, an infinitive verb.

Misinformed grammar snobs say that the "to" and the other half of the verb are like Kirk's good side and his evil side: They should never be separated. Thus, the meanies argue, that little word "boldly" comes between the inseparable "to" and "go"—a grammatical homewrecker.

On this basis, meanies think they can tell you where to put your adverbs. Some of the more clueless among them go so far as to say that you shouldn't break up any part of a compound verb. These people would actually have us say things like, "How has been Spock's health?" instead of "How has Spock's health been?"; or "I often have fantasized about Captain Kirk," instead of "I have often fantasized about Captain Kirk."

Happily for us, this "rule" has about as much authority as Chekov.

This little gem from the *Chicago Manual of Style* should put them in their place: "Although from about 1850 to 1925 many grammarians stated otherwise, it is now widely acknowledged that adverbs sometimes justifiably separate the 'to' from the principal verb. 'They expect to more than double their income next year.'"

Here's one from the *Associated Press Stylebook*: "Occasionally, however, a split is not awkward and is necessary to convey the meaning: 'He wanted to really help his mother.' 'Those who lie are often found out.'"

One more? Okay. Here's one from Strunk and White's *The*

Elements of Style: "Some infinitives seem to improve on being split, just as a stick of round stovewood does. 'I cannot bring myself to really like the fellow.' "

And that's from people so stuffy and old-timey that they actually thought it would be spot-on to make a reference to stovewood. So if these guys can lighten up enough to allow the occasional split infinitive, no half-baked meanie has a leg to stand on.

Avoid splitting your infinitives when possible, but split away when it sounds better to you. And if some windbag ever tells you that the famous *Star Trek* opening is grammatically incorrect, you can tell him to boldly blow it out his transporter. After that, you'll have no more tribble at all.

Chapter 5

The Sexy Mistake

"To Lay" versus "To Lie"

In an alarming abuse of police power, a team of Santa Monica officers stormed into a crime scene and ordered several suspected assailants to make love on the floor. How do I know this? Because I'm the editor who approved the story that ran in the newspaper. And once something appears in print, who am I to say it's untrue?

Of course, that wasn't the story I intended to run. I didn't even realize what I had printed until a reader called it to my attention.

"You meant to write, 'Police ordered the suspects to lie on the floor.' But you wrote, 'to lay.' I'm quite sure that the police did not tell the assailants to have sex." (I don't have the note from the reader, so I'm paraphrasing from memory. I may be getting his or her wording all wrong, but it's in print now, and therefore fact.)

A few years later I was in an airport shuttle bus in Paris. Two retired couples, Americans, were sharing the ride. Americans in Paris always seem really happy to meet each other. Perhaps that's because no one else seems too happy about our being there. Unfooled by my saucy beret and white-and-black-striped shirt, these nice people pegged me as a fellow Yank and struck up a conversation. One man asked what I did for a living. When I told him I was a copy editor, he lit up in a way that made it immediately obvious that he had a score to settle with his companions.

"Tell me: What are the most commonly confused words in the English language?"

"Oh," I answered very casually, " 'to lay' and 'to lie.' "

The man's face glowed in triumph as he gave a checkmating nod to his companions.

Honestly, I don't know why I came up with that answer or how it happened that he and I were on the same wavelength. I could have as easily said, "healthy and healthful," "bananas and plantains," or "religion and morality." But around 5:30 a.m. what popped out of my half-conscious brain was "to lay and to lie."

The difference between these two words is easy. Very easy. Setting aside the definition of "to lie" that means "to tell a fib," "to lie" is something I do to myself. "To lay" is something I do to something—or, ahem, someone—else. I lie on the beach. I lay the book on the table.

To use them correctly, you don't need to know that this is the difference between transitive and intransitive verbs. You don't need to know that a transitive verb requires a direct object, such as the book in the above example, or that an intransitive verb requires no object. For example, you don't need to know that the main definition of "to walk" is an intransitive verb because you can simply say, "I walk." But like a lot of verbs, "to walk" doubles as a transitive verb, because in a slightly different meaning of the word you might say, "I walk the dog." And you absolutely don't need to know that's why so many verbs in the dictionary have the abbreviations "vt," for "verb, transitive," and "vi," for "verb, intransitive." All you need to know to understand the difference between "to lay" and "to lie" is that the first one is done to something or someone else and the second one you do to yourself.

Of course, that's too easy. So there's a catch. The past tense of "to lie" just happens to be "lay." So, though you would say, "Today I lie on the beach," in the past tense you'd say, "Yesterday I lay on the beach." And from there, a whole world of confusion arises. For example, where does "lain" come in? And what or who, exactly, gets laid?

Don't be afraid. The other forms of these two words are also relatively easy. They are inflected (as the grammar books like to put it) as follows:

    lay-laid-laid
    lie-lay-lain

That means that both the past tense and the past participle of "lay" are "laid." "Today the suspects lay their guns on the floor." "Yesterday the suspects laid their guns on the floor." "At times the suspects have laid their guns on the floor."

Feel free to use the following mnemonic device to help you remember: "To lay is to get laid and laid." (This is meant in the stuffiest grammatical sense and in no way implies the kind of smut a Santa Monica police officer might read into it.)

"To lie," then, works as follows. "Today I lie on the beach." "Yesterday I lay on the beach." "At times, I have lain on the beach." None of those acts puts me in any danger of being arrested for lewd and lascivious behavior. But that's only because I conjugated the verb correctly.

I tried to explain this difference to the reporter who wrote the article. I explained "lay" versus "lie" and, in the process, mentioned that "lay" happens to be the past tense of "lie." That last bit of information might have confused him but, either way, he didn't get it.

"But when I wrote that police 'ordered them to lay,' that was in the past," he said.

That kind of blew my mind because suddenly the easy and intuitive process of putting actions into the past—something we all do every day without thinking—seemed like rocket science. My reporter friend was failing to see that he, himself, would never accidentally say, "I wanted to drove to the store," or "The teacher told them to thought about it."

We create verb phrases such as the ones above by adding a simple past tense of one verb—"told," "wanted"—to an infinitive of another verb—"to drive," "to think." The infinitive never changes.

Therefore, when you're talking about people lying on a floor, someone may have ordered them "to lie" on the floor. And yes, that's in the past tense. But the word after the "to" in the infinitive, in this case "lie," never changes. That's just how we make verbs, and it should not be confused with how Santa Monica police officers make headlines or how crime suspects make whoopee.

Chapter 6

Snobbery Up with Which You Should Not Put

Prepositions

In *The Elephants of Style*, author Bill Walsh reports that when he was five years old he enjoyed playing with alternate spellings of words. When I was five years old, I enjoyed playing in mud.

Word expert and "On Language" guest columnist Erin McKean proudly pronounced in one column, "I've wanted to be a lexicographer since I was eight." When I was eight, I wanted to be Donny Osmond's wife.

Punctuation stickler Lynne Truss looks back ruefully on age fourteen as a time when she tried to use big words to humiliate a pen pal. I look back ruefully on age fourteen as a time when I learned how to French inhale.

When it comes to troubled youth, the writing is always on the wall. And if someone doesn't recognize the signs and intervene, a disturbed kid has a lifetime of problems to look forward to. I'm talking about serious problems that, unlike dirty fingernails, smoking, and impure thoughts about Mormons, are unlikely to be corrected later in life.

Though some desperately uncool little word nerds manage to avoid the evil thrills of humiliating others through language, far too many find themselves caught in a vicious cycle of smug superiority and wedgies. Tragically, these youths blossom into adults whose sole pleasure in life comes from repeating clever but snooty lines such as Winston Churchill's defiant quip about the so-called rule that one should not end a sentence with a preposition: "That is the type of pedantry up with which I shall not put."

In some highly scientific research that consisted of me scratching my head and saying, "Gee, it sure seems like I've heard that a lot before," I have deduced that this Churchill quote is the single greatest thing ever to happen to meaniekind. Grammar snobs love it more than they love catching typos in the *New Yorker.* It's their favorite thing in the world, my science has shown.

Similarly scientific probability models have concluded that Churchill's highbrow tone and use of the word "pedantry" are the only reasons that meanies embrace loosening this rigid language "rule." Had Churchill expressed the same sentiment with words commonly used by people named Skeeter, the meanies would still demand that we say things like, "In whose oven are you going to bake that mud pie?" But today, even these nicotine- and Donny Osmond–deprived meanies concede it's okay to put the preposition "in" at the end: "Whose oven are you going bake that mud pie in?"

A quick refresher: Prepositions are little words like "about," "as," "at," "by," "for," "from," "in," "of," "on," "since," "through," "to," "toward," "until," "with," "without," etcetera—words that juxtapose certain actions or ideas with others. Some words are both prepositions and other parts of speech, such as "up." In "Put the book up on the shelf," "up" is a preposition. In "The baby can sit up," it's an adverb. If you need to distinguish between the two, just note that a preposition always takes an object: In the above example, "on the shelf" is the object of "up."

When it comes to putting prepositions at the end of sentences, the *Chicago Manual of Style* says, "The traditional caveat of yesteryear against ending sentences with prepositions is, for most writers, an unnecessary and pedantic restriction." (See, I told you they love words like "pedantry.")

The Elements of Style notes that, once upon a time, students were told not to end sentences with prepositions but that this "rigid decree" has loosened up over time. "Not only is the preposition acceptable at the end," Strunk and White write, "sometimes it is more effective in that spot than anywhere else. 'A claw hammer, not an ax, was the tool he murdered her with'"—a not-so-random example that would one day prove pivotal in convicting Mr. Strunk in a trial that inspired the Sherlock Holmes story "The Case of the Claw-Hammering, Homicidal Grammarian Who Eschewed the Ax."

Garner's Modern American Usage traces the nonrule back to its roots: "The spurious rule about not ending sentences with prepositions is a remnant of Latin grammar, in which a preposition was the one word that a writer could not end a sentence with."

Sassy how he ends that sentence with the preposition "with," huh?

Most people don't know that it's okay to end sentences with prepositions. The majority are haunted by vague memories of some teacher or other meanie harrumphing at a poor slob who said, "Who are you going to the movies with?" And the masses' insecurities are a boon to the meanies. As is their nature, grammar snobs are stuck in a cycle of forever salving old social hurts by grabbing every opportunity to feel superior, using others' weaknesses to their own advantage.

The snobs have even managed to twist the rules to give themselves free rein to break them while still insulting others who break them. For example, Strunk and White note, "Only the writer whose ear is reliable is in a position to use bad grammar deliberately."

And who, you might ask, gets to select the members of this secret Reliable Ear Society? Strunk and White don't say exactly, but they seem to think that reading their book will better your odds of being one of the chosen few.

Yes, obviously we're dealing with people still stinging from the humiliations of youth and getting their revenge on the cool cliques that rejected them by excluding pretty much the whole world from the Reliable Ear Society. Don't let them push you around. Your ear is better than they want you to know. End a sentence with a preposition anytime it sounds—to you—like the best alternative.

Chapter 7

Is That a Dangler in Your Memo or Are You Just Glad to See Me?

You're at the office. The vice president of passive-aggressive memos has just sent out his latest missive, an attack on one person disguised as a blanket edict for all. (He calls this leadership; everyone else calls it something that sounds like chickenship.) His memo is as follows:

> Despite our clearly defined policy regarding the breakroom coffeemaker, employees are still not taking responsibility for turning it off at night. Therefore, we're instituting a new policy regarding the use of the coffeemaker. From now on, everyone—not just the person who brewed the last pot but everyone—must check the coffeemaker before leaving at night. Clocking out every evening, the coffeepot should be in the forefront of your mind.

What do you do, hotshot? Do you:

A. Admit that you're the one who baked the black caffeine tar Mr. VP found still simmering in the pot when he came in yesterday morning;

B. Switch to tea;

C. Replace the framed photo of the VP's wife with an 8-by-10 glossy of a shirtless Tom Cruise; or

D. Undermine his authority by sending out a memo to all your co-workers making fun of the VP's dangler?

If you're like me, you know that not even revenge is worth breaking up your collection of Tom Cruise memorabilia. Thus the best option is D.: Expose the VP for the dangling dork that he is. Here's how.

Note the last sentence in his memo: "Clocking out every evening, the coffeepot should be in the forefront of your mind." Note that the coffeepot doesn't clock in or out (it's salaried). And voilà, you've spotted his small but clearly exposed little dangler.

"Dangling participle" may be the quintessentially alienating grammar term, at once intimidating, annoying, and memorable. It's a term normal people sometimes use to make fun of uptight grammar sticklers—an example of how ridiculously user-unfriendly grammar can be.

In fact, dangling participles and danglers in general describe what may be the single simplest rule of language: Make sense.

Consider these two sentences:

Panting in the heat, my shirt stuck to my body.

Stoned on Nyquil, the walls in my room seemed to be moving.

It doesn't take a master's degree in English to see there's something wrong here, though it often does require a post-graduate education to know that this very self-evident problem is termed a dangling participle.

A participle is pretty much what it sounds like—a piece of a multipart verb. Consider the multipart verbs "have walked" and "am walking." They consist of "auxiliary," or "helping," verbs— "have" and "am"—and a final part, usually ending in "-ing" or "-ed" or sometimes "-en." This final part is what's known as the participle.

For purposes of covering your dangler, you need only to think of participles as words ending in "-ing," "-ed" and "-en." So to avoid dangling, just take note every time you write a sentence that begins with one of these words. Then simply double-check to make sure that the person or thing performing the action in the second part of the sentence is the same person or thing that was performing the action described in the "-ing" or "-ed" verb in the first part of the sentence.

To make clear that it was not your shirt that was panting in the heat, write, "Panting in the heat, I felt my shirt sticking to my body."

To make clear that your walls, unlike you, always say no to Nyquil, write, "Stoned on Nyquil, I thought the walls were moving."

Sometimes the participles have shorter words such as "upon" before the "-ing," "-ed," or "-en" word:

Upon sending the memo, the staff knew that the vice president was a man of incredible java-related wisdom.

Technically, this sentence says that the staff sent the memo, when we know that really it was the VP. "While," "on," and "upon" are a few of the words that sometimes come into play in this way.

Dangling participles are probably the most common danglers, but there are other kinds, too. Happily, these are just as easy to understand and avoid:

A man of incredible vision, the coffeepot debacle was solved by the company vice president.

Even though the previous sentence does not begin with a participle, the man is dangling all the same. The above sentence should be:

A man of incredible vision, the company vice president solved the coffeepot debacle.

Or, even more precisely:

Formerly a man of incredible vision, the VP's eyesight was permanently blurred after an employee cracked a coffeepot over his head.

So of all the grammar terms you could fear, "dangling participle" should be at the bottom of your list. Despite how intimidating the term sounds, despite the intentions of any grammar snob who might try to use it to disarm you with his dazzling genius, it really is as simple as just remembering to make sense. And that's much easier than remembering to turn off the coffeemaker.

Chapter 8

An Open Letter to Someone Who Knows I Once Tried to Be a Grammar Snob but Failed

"Dreamed" versus "Dreamt," "Preventive" versus "Preventative," and Similar Pairs

Dear E.J. Whose Last Name I Forget:

You probably forgot me, too, but you and I went to middle school together. Then, about five years later, you and I also both worked at the local Kash n' Karry grocery store. One day in the break room you used the word "dreamt."

I said, " 'Dreamt' isn't a word. It's 'dreamed.' "

You said, "No. 'Dreamt' is a word."

I said, "Nuh-uh. It's 'dreamed.' "

You said, "No. 'Dreamt' is okay, too."

I said, "Nuh-uh. It's 'dreamed.' It's 'dreamed.' It's 'dreamed.' You're wrong."

At that point I think you turned your chair 180 degrees and struck up a conversation with the coffeemaker.

I know that was a long time ago, but I'm writing to apologize and to confess something: Even while I was saying all that stuff about "dreamed," I knew I might be wrong. I didn't really know if "dreamt" was a word or not. I just had a feeling that if I said, "You're wrong" over and over, eventually I'd win and you'd see that I could have been one of the cool kids in middle school all along.

Looking back, I still can't figure out why the "dreamed"/ "dreamt" thing seemed so important. It probably had something to do with the fact that when we were in middle school you dated Brenda B. even though my mom and I both agreed that I was prettier. (Actually my mom never met Brenda. But I know her taste and I'm pretty sure I could have had her vote.)

Anyway, I thought you'd like to know that about eighteen years later I finally looked up the word "dreamt." Turns out you were right. "Dreamt" is okay. My book says that British people often prefer "dreamt" and Americans prefer "dreamed," but they're both right. Sorry.

While I was in there (in the book, that is), I figured I might as well look up some other stuff I've been wondering about ever since our Kash n' Karry days. So I looked up "sneaked" and "snuck." I always thought that I understood this one, but now I see I was wrong here, too. Some people say "snuck" is okay, but most think it should be "sneaked."

Another one I looked up was "preventive" and "preventative." Turns out that the first one is right, the second one's considered not too smart. So I bet I used it at some point. Same for "cohabit." The extra syllable I put in sometimes, "cohabitate," is wrong. And same for "orient" versus "orientate"—the shorter one's better, at least in American English.

And since I just used the word "since," I should probably admit that the word "since" put me in my place recently, too. I always thought that "since" was only for time periods. So I thought "since last week " was okay, but "since you're going to be at the store anyway" was wrong and should be changed to "because you're going to be at the store anyway." I'm not sure how that idea got in my head, either. "Since" really is okay in place of "because," even though sometimes "because" is definitely better.

Anyway, if you'd have known me better during middle school, you might have noticed that I wasn't around during high school. I kind of dropped out, and, long story short, by the time we were working together at Kash n' Karry I was already planning on going back to school and already getting all college-headed or something. Yeah, something like that.

So I just wanted you to know that the whole "dreamt"/ "dreamed" thing made me realize I didn't want to be the kind of jerk who gets into arguments about stuff even though I know I have no idea what I'm talking about. Well, actually it took about ten years for me to just start to realize that. I spent a lot of years walking around all puffed up over how people would say "spit" when they should have said "spat." (Same for another word that rhymes with spit that I'm afraid I'll get in trouble if I say here.) But eventually the whole lesson from the stupid "dreamed"/"dreamt" fight sunk in. So if you find out about this book, don't tell people that I was once as hard-headed and ignorant as the people I'm ragging on and calling grammar snobs, k?

Thanks.

Stay as cool as you are.

June

Chapter 9

Anarchy Rules

"Adviser"/"Advisor," "Titled"/"Entitled," and Other Ways to Be Right and Wrong at the Same Time

In case I haven't said it lately, grammar snobs are great big meanies. In case you doubt it, I cede the floor to the accused.

Bill Walsh:

> Am I being elitist? Sure I am.
>
> I may be a curmudgeon.
>
> I may be strident on other points, but this is one where I truly believe that people who disagree with me are deranged.

Self-described grammatical stickler Lynne Truss:

> Grammatical sticklers are the worst people for finding common cause because it is in their nature (obviously) to pick holes in everyone, even their best friends. Honestly, what an annoying bunch of people.
>
> We are unattractive, know-all obsessives who get things out of proportion and are in continual peril of being disowned by our exasperated families.

Robert Hartwell Fiske (on Robert Hartwell Fiske): A "grumbling grammarian."

William Safire (on William Safire): An "excruciating curmudgeon."

James Kilpatrick, proudly self-proclaimed sovereign of his imaginary "Court of Peeves, Crotchets & Irks," on anyone who disagrees with him: "Pooh!"

William Strunk: Well, I don't have any dirt straight from the horse's mouth, but Stephen King sums up the late Strunk quite nicely as "that Mussolini of rhetoric." (And Stephen King likes the guy.)

As we continue to see, the problem with language today is that the people writing the rules are such blowhards that not even they themselves can deny it. There are no checks on their power. They declare themselves to be in a position to write rules, and then they do, without regard for the fact that other "authorities" before them have already written different rules. Language is left in a state of anarchy and you and I are left not knowing what to believe.

The contradictory rules that result are everywhere.

For example, on December 18, 2004, the *Los Angeles Times* reported that a director of national intelligence would be the "principal intelligence advisor to the president." On the same day, the Associated Press reported that the new director would be the principal "adviser."

The *Associated Press Stylebook*, a bible in some circles, is very clear on the use of the word "entitled": "Use it to mean a right to do or have something. Do not use it to mean 'titled.' Right:

'She was entitled to the promotion.' Right: 'The book was titled *Gone With the Wind*."

The equally venerable *Chicago Manual of Style* doesn't
tackle "entitled," but on page 124 the editors' position is made
clear in a sample letter that reads, "The University of Chicago
Press is pleased to undertake the publication of your contribu-
tion, entitled . . ."

The best-selling punctuation book *Eats, Shoots & Leaves*
tells you that a total of three apostrophes are needed in the expression "do's and don't's." *Webster's New World College Dictionary* recommends the inconsistent but cleaner "do's and
don'ts." The *Chicago Manual of Style* will tell you, however, to
lose yet another apostrophe: "dos and don'ts." Strunk and
White didn't bother to include the topic in their little book,
but the book's afterword by Charles Osgood makes specific
mention of "Strunk's do's and don'ts."

If you follow Strunk and White's rules on possessives, you
must write "Charles's friend." If you listen to AP, you must
write "Charles' friend."

As we'll examine in later chapters, these experts can't even
agree on how many commas go into "red, white, and blue,"
whether someone's age is "16" or "sixteen," or even whether to
write, "the '80s" or "the 80's."

A lot of these disputes have to do with style. For example,
the Associated Press sets the standard style for many newspapers, while the *Chicago Manual* writes the rules for books, the
Modern Language Association for academic papers, and so on.
Newspaper style tends to favor the efficient use of space,
which is why newspapers use numerals for ages: 16. But books
don't have to worry about that as much, which is why they spell
out ages: sixteen.

In a perfect world, it would stop there. But in the real world you have newspapers like the *Los Angeles Times* utterly affronted at the AP's suggestion that they spell "adviser" with an "e." Worse, you have newspapers like the *New York Times* utterly affronted by the suggestion that they should have to follow anyone else's rules whatsoever, which is why they're pretty much the only paper staffed by high school graduates in which you'll find an apostrophe in "the 1920's." This makes them look all the sillier when William Safire's "On Language" columns are compiled into book form, where his own published use of "1920's" is changed by the book editors to "1920s"—the exact same language column printed two different ways.

Of course, all this would be just a fascinating study of the behavior of wankers in their natural habitat were it not for the fact that they're screwing with the rest of us in the process. This grammar anarchy has created an environment in which anyone who wants to prove you or me "wrong" can cite multiple sources to put us in our place. But until now the best we could aspire to was a lame retort of, "Uh. That's debatable." So many ways to be wrong, so few ways to be right.

With friends like AP, *Chicago*, Kilpatrick, Safire, and the rest, English grammar needs no enemies. These are people who push the rest of us toward the edge, making us want to trash grammar entirely and begin allowing e-mail-speak such as "ICURrite" into corporate earnings reports and doctoral theses.

For damage control, grammar authorities try to justify their own existence by lecturing the rest of us about how important it is to speak and write good English. We've heard their spiel over and over again. "If you want to get ahead in almost any business or profession, you must speak and write reasonably correct English," writes Laurie Rozakis, author of *The Complete Idiot's Guide to Grammar and Style*.

It's a claim most of us can lay to rest with just two words:

Dan Quayle. Arguments such as Rozakis's also "misunderesti-mate" the forty-third president of the United States ("Is our children learning?"), they overlook the legendary Yogi Berra, and they fail to explain political newcomer Arnold Schwarzenegger, whose recent feats of communication include, "All of the politicians are not any more making the moves for the people, but for special interests." (Is it just me, or did anyone else wonder while watching *Terminator 2* why future generations would program a cyborg with a thick accent, then have the nerve to make the cyborg say that he continually learns from his environment?)

Ignorance of the language in no way hinders someone's ability to become wildly successful in politics or pro sports—we all knew that already. A lesser-known fact is that people who butcher the language can even rise to become professional wordsmiths. For example, a press release for a new Mattel toy some time ago said the new product would "strike a cord" between fathers and sons. People who write press releases some-times make quite a bit of money and often they're pretty well educated, or at least enough to know that there's no cord that connects fathers and sons. It should have been "strike a chord."

A photo by the Associated Press that appeared in the L.A. *Times* had a caption that said police told crowds of demonstra-tors to "disburse." Here you have one of the most respected names in the news business reporting that cops demanded that a group of protestors write them checks. They meant "dis-perse." Not to be outdone, the author and/or editor of one of the biggest-selling fiction books of all time, *The Da Vinci Code*, made the same mistake backwards. "His Holiness can disperse monies however he sees fit," author Dan Brown writes on page 175, suggesting an image of his fictional pope hurling fistfuls of euros from a hole in his Plexiglas popemobile.

One newspaper where I worked was somewhat famous for embarrassing flubs, especially ones that had to do with figures of speech. In this paper, there have been reports of people "ringing" others' necks (should have been "wringing"), living in a "doggy-dog" world (instead of the correct "dog-eat-dog" world), facing "a long road to hoe" (should have been "row to hoe"), driving "beamers" (the writer meant "Beemers"), yet not being "phased" by any of the goings on (should have been "fazed").

I've also seen professionals write "tow the line" and "set your sites." The first one is embarrassing because it should be "toe the line." The second one, however, is quite forgivable because, while it should have been "set your sights," as in the sights of a rifle, the not-so-well-paid professional who made that mistake was yours truly.

When the experts can't even get their stories straight and when professional writers make such egregious flubs, it's actually good news for the rest of us. It means that the seemingly huge gulf between ourselves and those in the know isn't so huge after all. It means that nine out of ten times when we're worried we don't know the right way to speak or write the experts don't know either. It means that our instincts are good and that common sense applies. It means that the super-arcane, super-difficult aspects of the language aren't things we're expected to know anyway. It means, in short, that this is our language too.

Chapter 10

The Comma Denominator

Good News: No One Knows How to Use These Things

Stop me if you've heard this one before. A panda walks into a café. No, wait. He goes to, um, uh, Niagara Falls. Yeah, that's it. And this panda walks directly up to the edge of the rushing water, where he allows himself to plummet over the side to the churning froth below, wildly gesticulating with his arms all the way down. The tragic suicide was a complete mystery to the panda's family until his wife came across a badly punctuated travel brochure in her husband's personal effects that said, "A visitor to Niagara sees, falls, and waves."

Yeah, yeah. I know: Groan. But you should be grateful I aborted my first play on *Eats, Shoots & Leaves*, which began, "A panda walks into a brothel . . ."

Those of you who don't spend your time scouring Books 'R' Us for the latest screed on punctuation might be surprised to learn that there's an entire book hinged on a little ditty about a panda. And if you question the seriousness of the threat posed by language meanies, get this: *Eats, Shoots & Leaves* has sold more than 1.1 million copies in the United

States, even though it was dedicated to British and not American style. Yup, more than a million Yanks stayed up into the late-night hours reading:

> This is probably the first thing you ever learn about commas, that they divide items in lists, but are not required before "and" on the end:
> > "The four refreshing fruit flavours of Opal Fruits are orange, lemon, strawberry and lime."

Riveting stuff, but at least it's useful, right? Don't answer until we take a look at Strunk and White's *The Elements of Style*:

> In a series of three or more terms with a single conjunction, use a comma after each term except the last. Thus write,
> > red, white, and blue
> > gold, silver, or copper
> > He opened the letter, read it, and made a note of its contents.

Moving on to the *Associated Press Stylebook*, the bible for most newspapers in the United States:

> Use commas to separate elements in a series, but do not put a comma before the conjunction in a simple series.
> > The flag is red, white and blue.
> > He would nominate Tom, Dick or Harry.

There's more. This from the revered *Chicago Manual of Style*, whose rules govern about ninety-nine out of a hundred books in your local bookstore.

> When a conjunction joins the last two elements in a series, a comma—known as the serial or series comma or the

Oxford comma—should appear before the conjunction.

> She took a photograph of her parents, the president,
> and the vice president.

Now, as we know from previous chapters, these people are all a bunch of wankers. But that doesn't mean we should dismiss the idea of learning how to confidently use a comma.

Besides, while clearly this disagreement over how to use the comma leaves you free to do whatever you want (most American authorities say to include the comma before the conjunction), some rules for using commas aren't so easily dismissed as mere matters of choice.

For example, what's wrong with the following sentence?

> The panda, whose wife still hasn't stopped laughing is the
> subject of a lawsuit against the management of Niagara
> Falls.

Yes, I know. Panda marriages aren't recognized in forty-nine states. (And of course we all hope that a constitutional amendment soon will make it an even fifty.) But did you also notice something funny going on with the commas? As Strunk, White, *Chicago*, AP, and even pandaphile Lynne Truss all agree, you need two commas to set off a parenthetical idea in a sentence. The missing comma in the above example should go after the word "laughing." Without that second comma it reads, ". . . laughing is the subject of a lawsuit." Sure, any reader can figure out what the sentence is supposed to mean, but the whole goal of punctuation is to make the written word as easy to understand as possible.

In the example with the panda's wife, the fact that she hasn't stopped laughing is a secondary point, an extra fact inserted into a sentence whose main point is something else entirely. You can lift it out completely and still maintain the integrity of the sentence's main point, that Mr. Panda is the subject of a lawsuit. That's why the clause about her laughing is considered "parenthetical." It's a subpoint, if you will. (The word "subpoint" is probably completely indefensible, but it works for me, so please indulge me.)

Sometimes, however, things that look like a subpoint are in fact crucial to the sentence because they make something in the main part clear. For example:

Pandas who visit Niagara frequently drown.

The "who visit Niagara" part isn't extra, you can't take it out and have the main point remain the same. "Who visit Niagara" is needed to make it clear that we're talking about a specific group of pandas—the ones who vacation at those fabulous falls. It would be wrong to say, "Pandas, who visit Niagara, frequently drown," because that would mean that all pandas visit Niagara. Again, ridiculous. We know that most pandas honeymoon on Maui.

The technical terms for these two scenarios, just so no one can yell at me for not putting them in here, are "restrictive clauses" and "nonrestrictive clauses." Others call them "essential" and "nonessential" clauses. A restrictive or essential clause narrows down the subject. It's the pandas who visit Niagara who are the ones drowning. The others—those who don't visit Niagara—die in barroom gunfights over missing punctuation. So if the extra information "restricts" the subject, narrows it down to a specific group or person, don't use the commas. If, on the other hand, you can lift the whole idea out of the sentence, keep the commas. Another illustration:

My sister, Mrs. Panda, lives off life insurance.

Here's something tricky that's good to know. The above is correct if I have only one sister. It says that Mrs. Panda *is* my sister—my only sister. If she's the only sister I have, her name is just extra information. Her name, in other words, is "non-restrictive"; it's not essential to understanding exactly who I'm referring to. But if I have more than one sister, a name is needed to make it clear which sister I'm talking about—restrictive. In that case, no commas, just, "My sister Mrs. Panda lives off life insurance. My sister Mrs. Koala subsists mainly on Foster's."

A lot of people get confused about the use of commas within sentences. For example, which is better?

On Tuesday I'm signing up with a panda dating service.

On Tuesday, I'm signing up with a panda dating service.

Most people don't know, so they wing it. They rely solely on their judgment, certain there's some rule they're ignorant of, when in fact the rule is to rely on your own judgment. Very short introductory clauses such as "on Tuesday" can go either way. Longer introductory clauses, such as, "Beginning on Tuesday and on every other Tuesday thereafter," should get a comma. But that's something most people don't need to be told.

When two parts of a sentence could stand alone as separate sentences but instead are glued together with "and," "but," or a similar word, then you're supposed to use a comma, my language books tell me:

I've read this many times, but I still can't seem to remember it.

I love pandas, and koalas aren't bad, either.

Without a conjunction such as "and" or "but," however, you either need a semicolon or you need to break up your sentence into two:

I've read this many times; I still can't seem to remember it.

There are twists and exceptions to these rules on commas, of course. For example, *Garner's Modern American Usage* tells us that when the two clauses are "closely linked," you don't need a comma: "Do as I tell you and you won't regret it."

But it all comes back to the question: Who gets to judge whether they're "closely linked"? You do.

The other super-obscure little rule on this usage is that when two objects share the same subject or subject and verb, you don't need a comma.

"I love pandas and koalas" is a shorter way of saying, "I love pandas and I love koalas." The subject and verb, "I love," are written out before "pandas" but they're implied before "koalas."

Perhaps the most perplexing use of the comma has to do with lists of adjectives. Consider the example, "He was a short, round, handsome panda." Commas work well between those adjectives. But everyone knows that you wouldn't put a comma between "bright" and "orange" in the sentence "He wore a bright orange hat." Well, there's an explanation for that. And yes, you guessed it, it's a vague explanation. So rather than mess it up by putting it in my own words, I'll leave it in Bryan Garner's: "If you could use 'and' between the adjectives, you'll need a comma," Garner writes, adding "When adjectives qualify the noun in different ways, or when one adjective qualifies a noun phrase containing another adjective, no comma is used. In these situations, it would sound wrong to use 'and'—e.g.: 'a distinguished (no comma) foreign journalist'; 'a bright (no comma) red tie.'"

I suspect this has something to do with why there's no

comma in *Grammar Snobs Are Great Big Meanies*, but don't quote me on that.

Of course, that's just Garner's way of understanding it. The *Chicago Manual* offers another explanation, Wilson Follett's *Modern American Usage* offers another—neither of which, in the big picture, do anything but add to the confusion. What all this amounts to, once again, is that there's no single "right" way and that nothing's better than instinct when it comes to understanding why "a tall, dark, handsome, confident man" might wear "a faded old floral luau shirt."

The final items on our list of "everything you always wanted to know about commas but were afraid to ask" are:

Yes, you should use a comma after, "Dear So-and-so," unless you prefer a colon.

Yes, commas are needed when attributing or setting up quotes. " 'I'm suing the publisher of the travel guide,' Mrs. Panda said." This rule is true regardless of whether the attribution comes before or after the quote. "Mrs. Panda said, 'I'll sue everybody.' " (When introducing long quotes, sometimes you might want to use a colon, but a comma is always a defensible choice, too.)

Yes, you make an exception when the quoted matter is part of the idea of the whole sentence. "The phrase 'I'll sue everybody' has become the mantra of the panda community."

Yes, when you have a comma before a year, you need one after the year.

Right: "The judge cited the July 14, 1996, case of *Panda v. Deep Pockets*."

Wrong: "The judge cited the July 14, 1996 case of *Panda v. Deep Pockets*."

Yes, too many commas in a sentence are a red flag that maybe you should break it up into multiple sentences.

And finally, yes, you can have hours and hours of fun pondering the importance of punctuation in sentences such as, "Woman panda without her man panda is nothing," versus "Woman panda: Without her, man panda is nothing." But you don't have to be in love with commas to know how to use them correctly or to avoid tumbling to your death at Niagara Falls.

Chapter 11

Semicolonoscopy

Colons, Semicolons, Dashes, Hyphens, and Other Probing Annoyances

Newspaper copy editors are perfectly normal people with good interpersonal skills. They are not weird or scary in any way. Their impressive expertise regarding the minutiae of grammar, word usage, and style in no way short-circuits the portions of their brains required for relating to other human beings. Copy editors never, ever remind me of the people whose neighbors will one day say of them things like, "Very quiet. Kept to himself mostly. Who knew he was capable of something like this?"

But while copy editors' language expertise does not detract from their warmth and charm, their wisdom does render this chapter utterly useless to them. You see, there's nothing in here that copy editors don't know already. With their already impressive mastery of this topic, they're certain to find nothing in here of any use. In fact, this is the chapter they'll find less interesting than any other in this book. No doubt their time could be better spent scouring the dictionary for typos or doctoring images of the local librarian in Photoshop.

They should all stop reading this chapter right now. Come to think of it, isn't there a *Star Trek* marathon on the Sci-Fi Channel right now?

There. That should've gotten rid of them.

They're gone now, right? Are you sure? Good. Thank God. Those guys give me the willies.

In fairness I should say, some of my best friends are newspaper copy editors. I should also probably note that the girl copy editors often seem more socially skilled than the boy copy editors. But that doesn't mean they all shouldn't be required to undergo a battery of psychological tests, if you know what I'm saying.

I don't know what makes many of them so very, very special. Ironically, it's not grammar snobbery. On the contrary, these men and women know enough about language to know that nobody knows "enough" about language.

In fact, when I made the move from working at a press-release distribution service into a real newspaper's newsroom, I was floored to see how these pros handle questions from reporters and colleagues—questions such as, "Is 'website' one word or two?" Unlike many of us at the press-release service who would quickly volunteer our genius by speculating and debating such questions, real newspaper copy editors reach for a book. They have no desire to flaunt their knowledge. They have nothing to prove. They'd rather give you the correct answer than impress you with pulling one out of their own brains. And for that, my hat's off to them.

But in other ways, they're just . . . just . . . well, here's an example.

A reporter at the newspaper where I worked wanted to know why someone kept changing her semicolons to colons. This reporter had always been rather proud of her mastery of the semicolon, so one day she noticed a change to one of her sentences that had read something like, "Parking is the main concern; Rutter favored an alternative with 375 spaces."

This sentence showed up in the paper with a colon in place of that semicolon. My friend decided that perhaps her grasp of the semicolon wasn't as hot as she'd always thought; she let the colon-switch slide. Then it happened again. Then again. Baffled, she launched an officewide e-mail that in turn launched an officewide debate. Eventually, one of us looked it up in the *AP Stylebook*:

> In general, use the semicolon to indicate a greater separation of thought and information than a comma can convey, but less than the separation that a period implies.

That's what she had been doing.

Still, the copy editor in question (who was the subject of much speculation in our office because he was the only person there who carried a briefcase and no one ever, ever saw him open it) didn't see it her way.

Colons, according to the AP, "often can be effective in giving emphasis. 'He had only one hobby: eating.'"

And that's what our scary, briefcase-toting friend believed that the reporter wanted to say.

Carefully conducting the discussion in the safe public forum of intra-office e-mail, she explained to the copy editor that the semicolon better reflected the intention of her sentence. And, call me crazy, but it seems to me that the writer is in a better position to determine the intent of her own work.

Mr. Mystery Briefcase acquiesced. In the e-mails, he agreed that questions of whether to use a colon, semicolon, or dash are often just judgment calls. He conceded that her interpretation of her own words was at least as valid as his.

So you can imagine our surprise when, not long after, her semicolons again began to be mysteriously replaced by colons.

She let it slide, which may be why she's alive and well today.

* * *

Besides separating thoughts, colons and semicolons also play an important role in lists. One of the most common uses for colons is to introduce lists. "The felony charges against the killer known as Mr. Mystery Briefcase are as follows: assault, battery, and semicolonicide."

In lists and elsewhere, semicolons are basically über-commas. They help separate things that are really long and cumbersome or that are already bogged down with commas: "His home contained a collection of shrunken heads, which were thought to have been obtained legally; a collection of normal-sized heads, which police think were probably obtained illegally; and copies of numerous magazines considered to be evidence, including *The Recluse*, *Shack and Garden*, and *Bon Appétit*."

As you can see from the example above, semicolons can sometimes be a clue that you should be breaking things up into shorter sentences. But other times, they're the way to go.

Dashes are equally flexible. They can signal an abrupt change in thought or tempo of speech. But in this way, they're at times interchangeable with the colon, as in the example above. "He had only one hobby—eating."

Dashes are also good for setting off ideas or lists or groups within a sentence. And this, of course, makes them a lot like commas. "The expert witness listed the qualities—reclusiveness, social awkwardness, and irrational outbursts—common in more violent copy editors."

The only other time I dared to tangle with a newspaper copy editor, it was also over colons. The rules say that, if what follows a colon is a complete sentence, it should begin with a capital letter. "He showed me his shrunken head collection: It scared me." Otherwise, no capital. In this particular instance I had written something like, "Friends told the reporter what to do: Get a gun." The copy editor changed the "G" to lower-case, saying that "get a gun" wasn't a complete sentence because it did not contain a subject. Here's what I did not say: "Get a gun" is a complete sentence because in imperative sentences (commands) the subject is implied. In the above example, it's "you," as in, "You get a gun."

In my disagreement with the copy editor, I knew I was holding a winning hand. But I folded anyway. Survival instinct had told me to keep my mouth shut, and perhaps that's why I lived to tell.

Chapter 12

The O.C.: Where the '80s Never Die

Lessons on the Apostrophe from
Behind the Orange Curtain

There's a Piaget or Rolex on your wrist. A Mercedes is parked in your driveway. You've never heard of grunge and you actually believe that the pursuit of money is a worthwhile way to spend your life. Quick: What year is it?

If you said 1986 you are correct. If you said present day, you're correct only if you're living in *The O.C.*—Orange County, California, of bad TV fame.

My grammar column and hence my pretending to know something about grammar both originated in a little section of the *Los Angeles Times* that covers just Newport Beach and Costa Mesa, California. Newport Beach is the subject of *The O.C.*; Costa Mesa is the city next door that's less glamorous, more diverse, and thus completely ignored. My column came into being shortly before the Fox show launched Newport Beach into a dubious brand of fame as a place where '80s self-indulgence lives on oblivious to time, global realities, and the dot-com crash.

Had my column appeared in the *New York Times* instead of a section of the *Los Angeles Times*, one of the most notable differences—besides the fact that I wouldn't have this fabulous Marissa-like tan—would be that I would write "the 80's" instead of "the '80s."

Why? Because, as you've seen by now, language rule-makers are conspiring to drive the rest of us nuts. In this case the culprit is the *New York Times*, which bizarrely insists on defying conventional wisdom on this matter. Pretty much every other major newspaper in the country is perfectly happy using an apostrophe to replace the "19" or "18" in a year, such as shortening "the 1980s" to "the '80s." What's more, most other outlets agree that there should be no apostrophe before the "s." "The 1980s."

As we saw in chapter 9, the Gray Lady begs to differ. In her realm, even language meanie William Safire's name appears above such bizarrely punctuated phrases as, "Disraeli seems to have said it in the 1830's." The *New York Times* does this despite the Associated Press's clear instruction to add only the "s" without the apostrophe: "Flappers did their flapping in the 1920s." This is the general rule for any number made plural, as AP illustrates: "The airline has two 727s. Temperatures will be in the low 20s. There were five size 7s." No apostrophes in any of those cases.

So the *New York Times* does a complete flip-flop on other major papers' practice of putting an apostrophe before the decade but not after: 80's instead of the more accepted '80s. But the paper hasn't cornered the market on apostrophe insanity. Far from it. In a January 18, 2005, front-page story, the *Los Angeles Times* wrote about a student "who earns A's and Bs in community college."

This was not an accident; it was as deliberate and methodical as any jauntily tied sweater around the shoulders of an Izod shirt—a popular look in the '80s. The *Los Angeles Times* editors were trying to follow the general logic that says the apostrophe is mainly for possessives and omissions—that the only other time you should use it is when to omit the apostrophe would create confusion or especially when it would spell another word—"a" plus "s" equals "as"; "b" plus "s" gives us a much better hint as to what's going on here, but it doesn't technically spell a word. Hence the *Los Angeles Times*'s using an apostrophe for "A's" but none for "Bs."

Once again this is a case of a newspaper thumbing its nose at the idea it should follow anyone's rules but its own: The *Associated Press Stylebook* says to use apostrophes when naming single letters: "Mind your p's and q's." "He learned his three R's and brought home a report card with four A's and two B's." "The Oakland A's won the pennant."

Of course, even AP can't resist jerking us around a little in its very next entry, which deals with multiple letters. Suddenly, their yes-apostrophe rule becomes a no-apostrophe rule, with no explanation for the switch. "She knows her ABCs." "I gave him five IOUs." "Four VIPs were there."

It's enough to make even those MBAs who got A's want to plow their BMWs into some language VIPs.

Not yet infuriated to the max? Then consider this: *Eats, Shoots & Leaves*, which has a whole chapter on the apostrophe and whose author has ties to something called the Apostrophe Protection Society (which in turn has ties to radical groups the Comma Crusaders, the Hyphen Hezbollah, and the North American Maniacal Bracket Lovers' Association), says the apostrophe should be used to make the plurals of words you're referring to as words. For example, author Truss notes, it should be: "Are there too many but's and and's at the beginnings of sentences these days?" The AP—surprise, surprise—gives contradictory advice to skip the apostrophe: "His speech had too many 'ifs,' 'ands' and 'buts.'" Just for fun, the AP people mention that their rule is an exception to *Webster's New World College Dictionary*, which is AP's own fallback reference.

And as we saw in chapter 9, no matter whether you write "do's and don't's," "do's and don'ts," or "dos and don'ts," two out of three language authorities will tell you you're wrong.

At this point, those of you who tuned in for some insight into the O.C. have endured more than enough abuse. And because I still owe you a little something SoCal, here at last is the inside scoop on the real O.C., abridged version: Never trust TV. Here's my expanded explanation: You know how on the TV show the people are always beautiful and well dressed and disproportionately members of just one race? Well, of course that's not accurate. Real-life Newporters are just as beautiful and homogenous, but many of them don't dress to flaunt the bucks—conspicuous consumption is so *nouveau riche*. Besides, it could get you mugged if you venture east of South Coast Plaza.

Oh, and one more thing about *The O.C.*—much of that gorgeous scenery is shot not in the gated Newport Beach community of Newport Coast where the TV families supposedly live, but in stunning locales in Los Angeles County's South Bay area. Thus, the O.C. you see is no more real than rules on apostrophes.

Chapter 13

Go Ahead, Make Up Your Own Words

Prefixes and Suffixes and Why the Dictionary Thinks You're Wrong

I hope that, by this point, you're feeling a little less intimidated by the meanies, because I've got some bad news: Meanies come in many forms, not just human. They can be not only animal, but also mineral. In rare cases, they can even be vegetable, but we can talk about William F. Buckley some other time. Right now, I'd rather focus on that most useful assembly of minerals, the computer. More specifically, I'm talking about spell-checker. And, more specifically yet, I'm talking about how, when it comes to suffixes and prefixes, even Bill Gates's best and brightest aren't the boss of you.

Check it out.

A minute ago, "overmoneyed" was not a word. Now it is. Why? Because I say so. Here it is used in a sentence: "Warren Buffett is overmoneyed." Okay, I didn't say "overmoneyed" was a good word. Nor did I say I'd be able to come up with a good sentence to use it in. But "overmoneyed" is a good example of how your knowledge and instincts are better than the meanies—man or machine—would have you believe.

You see, just a few paragraphs into typing this chapter my computer screen is already littered with rather nasty-looking little red squiggles, courtesy of Gates and co., silently screaming that "overmoneyed" is not found in my software's spell-checker. I once received a similar slap from a reader of my column who fumed at my use of the word "nonword." "It's not in the dictionary!" the meanie complained. Yet despite my computer's crimson criticism, "overmoneyed" is as legitimate a word as "spell-checker," with which the techies who programmed this machine seem to have no problem.

"With few exceptions, the prefix 'non-' does not take a hyphen unless it is attached to a proper noun," Bryan Garner says.

So despite the reader's rather over-the-top wailing, "nonword" is defensible, too.

That's the whole point of prefixes and suffixes—they're little pieces you attach to other words to make your own meaning. And their magic is that they allow you to create legitimate words not found in spell-checker or even in the dictionary.

Try it yourself. Open up a new document on your computer, then look around the room. What do you see? I mean, besides half of last week's tuna sandwich and those magazines you have to hide before your mom comes over for a visit. Do you see any books by William F. Buckley? No? Then your room is antiblather. Have you removed that week-old sandwich yet? If not, your room may contain tunaborne bacteria.

Now type those two words into your computer. See the angry red squiggles? (For those of you smart and rebellious enough to have resisted indoctrination into the Cult of We Who Live to Enrich Lord Gates, I can only guess what you might be seeing. But I bet it's smarter and more user-friendly than the stuff on my screen.) Those judgmental and jagged red lines need intimidate you no more. Thumb your nose at them by trying a couple more new words.

Check your pocket. Is there any change in there? If not, you'd probably already be comfortable saying you're penniless, but now you can write with complete confidence that you're also dimeless and quarterless. (Hey, little red lines: Go squiggle yourselves.) Does your room have windows? If so, it's ventilat-able. (Should that be spelled by leaving the "e" in before the "-able" part? No one knows. We just made the word up. So we're the authority on the subject and we say no.) Are there dust bunnies under your bed? No? Then you may be a hyper-sweeper.

Make up some more using this sampling of prefixes and suffixes I pilfered off the Internet, mostly from websites that contain the phrase "Grades 3 to 5" yet still seemed a bit over my head.

> **Prefixes:** a-, un-, co-, omni-, re-, sub-, pre-, bi-, mis-, dis-, inter-, anti-, pro-, non-, mono-, de-, hypo-, hyper-, mal-, retro-, trans-, poly-, ob-, ab-, semi-, equi-, epi-, over-, ab-, ad-, com-, ex-, in-.

> **Suffixes:** -y, -est, -ence, -able, -ible, -ship, -ance, -al, -ish, -or, -er, -ment, -tial, -ist, -ism, -ency, -sion, -tion, -ness, -hood, -dom, - en, -ify, -ize, -ate, -worthy, -wide, -tic, -less, -tive, -ous, -ful, -tial, -ly, and my personal favorite, -tude.

But June, you might say, a lot of the possible combinations look really funny, like "strip clubwide," "antiinebriation," and "coorganizer." Wouldn't a hyphen or something make them prettier? Ah, I would reply, stroking the place on my chin where a beard would be if I were a wise master and you were called "Grasshopper," your instincts are good ones. Then, to demonstrate just how smart you are, I would tell you to wax my car while blindfolded. Of course you'd be too smart for that, laughing out loud as you waved a carefully selected finger in my face, thereby proving my point that you should trust your instincts.

The experts—the meaniest among them—concede that there are no hard-and-fast rules. They offer some general guidelines that, while useful, still leave plenty of room for disagreement and debate. Before we look at the written guidelines, let's just see what your eye tells you by comparing the following pairs:

> "strip clubwide" or "strip-club-wide"
> "antiinebriation" or "anti-inebriation"
> "coorganizer" or "co-organizer"

If you chose the second examples, you're either quite good at this or you're already familiar with the lingo because you work as assistant manager at one of those places that offer nude nudes but do not serve liquor.

Here are the guidelines that are basically just an extension of what you already sense.

When you're adding a prefix to create a word that's not already in the dictionary, normally you should not use a hyphen. It's the opposite with suffixes: When you're using one to make a word not in the dictionary, most often you do add a hyphen.

There are some exceptions, then there are exceptions to the exceptions, then there's a no-man's-land in which the experts themselves don't dare to tread because there are no rules, only judgment calls. Here are the most useful guidelines. Follow these whenever spell-checker or the dictionary do not contain the word you want to make up.

For prefixes, use a hyphen when:

- adding on to a capitalized word or a numeral: anti-American, pre-1950s (which just reaffirms your instincts that "antiAmerican" and "pre1950s" look ridiculous, right?)
- putting two vowels together: "pro-occult," "anti-illness" (again, you already knew not to use "prooccult" or "antiillness")
- adding a prefix to an expression that's already hyphenated: "non-self-serving." An annoying glitch: Expressions containing more than one word but that are not hyphenated such as "Civil War" use something called an "en dash" to connect the prefix. An "en dash" is basically what you'd get if a hyphen and a regular dash (known as an "em dash") had a baby together. They're kind of long, kind of short, and they're indistinguishable from hyphens to everyone except book-publishing editors. What's more, en dashes don't exist at all in the newspaper world. So if you're like me, you can muddle through life happily oblivious to en dashes and use hyphens instead until the day your publisher sends back your edited manuscript pointing out that you need to get a clue about en dashes—and fast.

So, back on topic, you'd write "post–Civil War" with an en dash because, unlike "self-serving," "Civil War" is not hyphenated. Again, that's only if you're trying to comply with book-publishing rules. Otherwise, a hyphen's fine. The important thing to remember here is that prefixes need some sort of squiggle to connect them to multiword compounds. Consider the alternatives, "nonself-serving" and "postCivil War," and the choice becomes a no-brainer.

- using the prefix "co-": "Co-" is an oddball because unlike most prefixes it normally does require a hyphen. Exceptions include widely accepted words such as "coexist," "cooperate," and "coordinate."
- using the prefix "post-": "Post-" is another oddball in that it customarily takes a hyphen except for some widely accepted words such as "postdate," "postdoctoral," "postelection," "postgraduate," "postscript," and "postwar."

Unlike prefixes, suffixes usually take a hyphen; "-free," as in "oil-free," is a good example of how suffixes seem to beg for hyphens. Make exceptions for:

- the suffix "-like": "ratlike," except for words ending in "l"—"weasel-like"
- "-borne": yup, you can really say "tunaborne bacteria" if you like.
- "-wide": You'd say "officewide" and "countrywide"; make exceptions for long words or whenever skipping a hyphen creates confusion: "United States of America-wide."

As instinct tells you, use a hyphen with any prefix or suffix that would otherwise create confusion, like with "re-create" versus "recreate."

No matter what, if a meanie tries to tell you something is not a word just because it's not in the dictionary or in spell-checker, tell him he's just suffering from superanalness.

Chapter 14

Hyphens: Life-Sucking, Mom-and-Apple-Pie-Hating, Mime-Loving, Nerd-Fight-Inciting Daggers of the Damned

Now that I've warned you about newspaper copy editors and about how hyphens wreak havoc with prefixes and suffixes, I feel you're ready to entertain another dose of horror: Somewhere out there, at this very moment, two copy editors are having an argument that sounds something like this:

"You had no right to put a hyphen in the story I edited about the orange juice salesman."

"You should have hyphenated it. In that context, 'orange' and 'juice' are forming a compound modifier and therefore require a hyphen. 'Orange-juice salesman.'"

"But reasonable use dictates that 'orange' and 'juice' form a familiar compound, one a reader can recognize without the hyphen."

"But without the hyphen, it's not clear whether you're

talking about a man who sells orange juice or an orange man who sells some other kind of juice."

"Oh yeah? Well . . . your mama dangles her participles!"

As you can see, the hyphen is a nasty, tricky, evil little mark that gets its kicks igniting arguments in newsrooms and trying to make everyone in the English-speaking world look like an idiot—it's the Bill Maher of punctuation.

This is true because hyphenation is in a state of anarchy. Most people don't know how to use hyphens, and those who do keep making up their own rules as they go along. The hyphen is in such a pickle that you could easily argue it's time to trash the whole system, perhaps rewrite the rule to say, "Hyphens are to be used whenever the writer thinks they look good and are not required otherwise." But before you start a grassroots campaign to flush the whole business, consider this: Without the diversion of arguing about hyphens, thousands upon thousands of people just like the two above could end up with nothing better to do than to cruise your local bar trying to land a date—with you.

Copy editors need hyphens like prison inmates need cigarettes and Karl Rove needs pentagrams and babies' blood.

Hyphenation is the first thing a lot of copy editors learn in their trade. The basic rule of hyphens—the first thing these eager young copy editors learn—is that they're used to form compound modifiers, that is, to link two or more words that are acting as adjectives or sometimes adverbs.

The sentence, "The mime-punching clown went on a killing spree," illustrates the way in which the hyphen helps your eye better see the writer's meaning. Without the hyphen, you see "mime punching" and you wonder whom the mime is punching. But with the hyphen, you can see that it is the clown who's doing the punching—punching mimes, for which we are all grateful.

So, while "orange juice" doesn't take a hyphen, this rule dictates that it should when it's modifying "salesman."

The problem is, about half the copy editors in the world think that "orange-juice salesman" looks ridiculous. So they don't do it, citing rules such as the *Oxford English Grammar*'s "a hyphen is inserted if it is needed to clarify which words belong together" as some newsroom equivalent of, "Go ahead. Make my day." As a result we see *Eats, Shoots & Leaves* author Lynne Truss subtitling her book *The Zero Tolerance Approach to Punctuation*, and indeed skipping the hyphen in "zero tolerance."

There's an important exception to the compound-modifier rule: It doesn't apply to adverbs ending in "-ly." The idea here is that the "-ly" in "happily married couple" makes it clear that "happily" modifies "married" and not "couple." Fair enough.

Many words also include hyphens in their official spelling; the only way to know which ones they are is to check a dictionary. But prepare for pain. In the dictionary, you're likely to see that "water-ski" is a verb but the noun describing the equipment itself is "water ski." The person doing the skiing, by the way, is always a "water-skier." So, the water-skier water-skis on water skis. In the dictionary, you may also learn that an air conditioner air-conditions to provide air conditioning. Or perhaps that a virus can be airborne and also wind-borne.

Told you the little buggers were evil.

Despite how invidious hyphens can be, their main purpose is to help you. For example, if you want to write about a person who is creating something for a second time, but this comes out as "recreate," which means to relax and have fun, throw in a hyphen: "re-create." Same is true for a "recovering" (getting healthier) and "re-covering" (covering again), as in re-covering your sofa. If you want to write about someone entering a place a second time, but "reenter" looks too weird, again, throw in a hyphen: "re-enter."

But what about all those other uses for hyphens we've all seen a million times and never thought about: head-butted, copy-edit, crop-dusting, multi-ethnic, cross-reference, two-thirds? Well, they're all just evidence that the hyphens are life-sucking, mom-and-apple-pie-hating, mime-loving, nerd-fight-inciting daggers of the damned.

Therefore, whenever you're faced with the question of whether to hyphenate something, ask yourself the following question: Do I want to be "right" by normal people's standards, or do I need to be right-right, as in, must-withstand-the-slings-and-arrows-of-evil-hyphen-mavens right?

If you only need to know the basics, here's what you do:

1. Hyphenate all compound modifiers before a noun except ones with "-ly" adverbs, and except when to hyphenate them seems stupid, such as in "orange juice salesman."

2. Hyphenate all fractions and hyphenate numbers between "twenty-one" and "ninety-nine," including when they're part of larger numbers such as "two hundred ninety-nine."

3. For all other words, check the dictionary, paying special attention to whether the definition refers to a noun, verb, or adjective.

4. Don't be self-conscious about your hyphens, especially in business correspondence. It's a waste of time. The chance that some suit will scoff when he sees

"freelance" not hyphenated on your résumé is just as good as the chance that he'd scoff at "free-lance" with a hyphen. His judgment could be based on something as arbitrary as which version of the *Associated Press Stylebook* is sitting on his desk. Prior to 2004, "free-lance" required a hyphen, according to that reference guide. But as of 2004, it's "freelance." Go figure. Regardless, if the guy in the expensive suit in the big office is looking for something wrong, he will find it, whether you were "wrong" or not. But if he has any amount of experience under his belt, he's probably wise enough to take these little things in stride.

If you really need to know your stuff with hyphens, the rest of this chapter is for you.

The first thing you should do is buy an absurd number of books on the subject, read them over and over in a vain attempt to find some common ground, go berserk, and embark on a tri-state killing spree.

In prison, you'll have a lot of time to decide which of these books is the camp you're going to join. If you're really into pain, I suggest the *Chicago Manual of Style*. After two pages of general guidelines for hyphenation and forming other compounds, *Chicago* lists sixty-six specific guidelines for everything from "age terms" (e.g., "three-year-old") to "Web" (e.g., "Web site," "Web-related matters," "Web happy").

Since they're going nuts anyway, the *Chicago* folks figured, why leave simple rules alone? For example, the word "tuna-borne" we created in chapter 13 was an example of a slightly annoying but not unreasonable rule: that "-borne" is an exception to the rule to hyphenate most suffixes. And if you thought it was bad enough that the grammar snobs expected you to memorize rules for specific suffixes such as "-borne," consider the "help" offered by the *Chicago Manual*: "borne: 'water-borne,' 'foodborne,' 'cab-borne,' 'mosquito-borne.' (Normally closed, but hyphenated after words ending in *b* and after words of three or more syllables.)"

Chicago's sixty-six hyphenation rules don't include prefixes, by the way. That's why there are another thirty-seven entries just for prefixes such as "extra-" (" 'extramural,' 'extrafine,' but 'extra-administrative' ") and "mega-" ("hyphenate before words beginning with an 'a.' ")

Still determined to "learn" hyphenation? Then you might want to take note of the fact that the compound-modifier rule refers mostly to stuff that comes before a noun. After a noun, hyphens often are not needed. A *well-known* musician is *well known*.

Would you like some infuriating exceptions? You got 'em. Compounds so common they appear in the dictionary, terms like "good-looking," keep their hyphens regardless of whether they come before or after a noun. *Good-looking* people are *good-looking*.

You're still reading? You really want another exception? One that's hotly debated among authorities and sure to prove that you can't please all the snobs all the time? Okay.

Some books will tell you that compounds with words ending in "-ed," such as "strong-willed," are hyphenated regardless of whether they come before the noun. For example, *Oxford* says that you should always hyphenate "middle-aged," "short-haired," "strong-willed," "long-winded," "tight-lipped," and "queen-sized"—a list that reads as if they compiled it by reading archived stories about the 1998 presidential impeachment.

So, according to *Oxford*, Bill Clinton is middle-aged, short-haired, strong-willed, and long-winded. Monica Lewinsky is queen-sized and not very tight-lipped.

The *Chicago Manual of Style* disagrees with *Oxford*'s rule, saying that "-ed" compounds are hyphenated only before the noun. But their advice seems impractical in the above example: "Bill Clinton is middle aged, short haired, strong willed, and long winded while Monica is queen sized and not very tight lipped." I miss the hyphens almost as much as I miss the days when Nixon was the closest any president had come to being impeached in my lifetime.

Still determined to "know" hyphenation? Then don't forget to memorize all the rules in chapter 13 of this book, which deals specifically with prefixes and suffixes and when to hyphenate them. Oh, and you might want to bone up on the various rules governing numbers. For example, there's never a hyphen before the word "percent" in things like, "a 12 percent chance," but there's always a hyphen when the number and another word are modifying a third word, as in, "a hundred-page document." Ages expressed with "-year-old," as in "ten-year-old" always take hyphens.

If you're the type of person who is still reading even after all those maddening hurdles, you might find the following trick a little fun (a warning sign if there ever was one). Lists of hyphenated things can be treated as follows: "The haircuts look good on long- and short-haired women alike." AP calls this "suspensive hyphenation." *Oxford* refers to it as "linking," and *Chicago* calls it "hyphen with word space."

Once you've served out your entire prison term, during which you devoted every non-shiv-making moment to hyphenation, you still won't know one hundred percent of the time how to use hyphens. You'll just have a better idea of which book to open when you have a question.

Painful stuff? Yes. But it's still better than fighting off advances from guys who get their jollies arguing about the color of juice salesmen.

I'll Take "I Feel Like a Moron" for $200, Alex

When to Put Punctuation Inside Quotation Marks

"Yes, I'll take 'Easy Things That Are Difficult Only for Me' for $500, Alex."

"Here is your clue: A garment you wear on your head."

"What is a sock, Alex?"

"No, I'm sorry. We were looking for 'hat.' Next answer: This first president of the United States now appears on the one-dollar bill."

"Who is Walt Disney?"

"Oh, sorry, no. Now will you please get your dolt carcass off my set and go get some moron job such as writing for a TV sitcom?"

"Of course, Alex. I'm so sorry to have wasted your time like this, Alex. I'll just crawl under a rock and die now, Alex."

That is pretty much how I feel every time I watch *Jeopardy!* I like to blame my lousy education—and it truly was lousy. But I'm not sure how different things would be had I received a quality education. I have a good brain for some things, but facts like names and places and titles just don't stick in my head. History is especially troubling. I'm still not sure who fought in the Spanish-American War or when the War of 1812 took place.

This brand of brain deficiency is particularly embarrassing because of the company I keep. I've always had a lot of smart friends, and they always think I'm one of them until we're in a room with a TV broadcasting Alex Trebek's patronizing personage.

But one day recently, I was finally able to declare an end to *Jeopardy!*'s tyrannical abuse of my intellectual self-esteem and announce the greatest victory of my life, perhaps the single greatest achievement of humankind: I knew something that the people who produce *Jeopardy!* did not.

On a recent episode, Alex posed a question that ended with this phrase, written exactly as follows: *"over the arc"*, *so to speak*.

After the Mormon Tabernacle Choir stopped singing in my head, I realized that I had no reason to declare a triumph. The placement of the comma outside the quotation marks was probably just a typo. And everyone makes typos.

Then, it happened: They did it again, in the same episode even. A second time they placed a comma outside of the quotation marks.

It turns out that the *Jeopardy!* writers make this mistake so habitually that a *Parade* magazine reader actually wrote about it in the "Ask Marilyn" column.

Now listen up, Alex, and listen good: In American English, the period and the comma always go inside the quotation marks. Always. Semicolons always go outside the quotation marks. For all other punctuation marks it depends on the context. As the *Associated Press Stylebook* puts it, "The dash, the semicolon, the question mark and the exclamation point go within the quotation marks when they apply to the quoted matter only. They go outside when they apply to the whole sentence."

Say you're recounting an imaginary conversation that took place only in your head in which you said, "Now don't you feel inferior to me, Alex?" When you send out a group e-mail to all your friends, you might say, "So I looked that Trebek guy right in the eye and said, 'I'm clearly much smarter than you. Don't you feel inferior?'"

One or all of your friends or even your therapist might reply: And how does it make you feel to tell someone, "I'm smarter than you"?

Notice that in the first case the question mark is inside the quotation marks because the thing being quoted is actually a question. But in the second case, the real question being asked is about the quote, not within the quote.

So now if you'll just give me my $11,400 in winnings (my own rough estimate of this victory's monetary value) and concede that I've evolved beyond having to know things like the location of the Mississippi River or the name of the first symphony written by Beethoven, I'll be on my way now, Alex.

Chapter 16

A Chapter Dedicated to Those Other Delights of Punctuation

This chapter is dedicated to those other delights of punctuation—exquisite little squiggles, those most delightful dots and dashes, and other tragically underappreciated tiny tidbits!

Nah. I'm just yankin' your chain.

But I did recently read a whole book on the history, trivia, and borderline erotic appeal of punctuation marks—research into a world so bizarre that it made me want to write off punctuation altogether. Consider the following from *Eats, Shoots & Leaves*: "Using the comma well announces that you have an ear for sense and rhythm, confidence in your style and a proper respect for your reader, but it does not mark you out as a master of your craft. But colons and semicolons—well, they are in a different league, my dear! They give such lift!" author Truss writes. "The humble comma can keep the sentence aloft all right, like this, UP, for hours if necessary, UP, like this, UP, sort-of bouncing, and then falling down, and then UP it goes again."

Is it just me, or does this sound to you like a subconscious cry for Viagra? Yes, eventually the author does tear herself away from talking about the comma and get to her original point about colons and semicolons. Surprise: She loves them. It would be fun to pit her in a death match with *Lapsing into a Comma* author Bill Walsh, whose passion for the semicolon is just as strong, albeit in the opposite direction. "The semicolon is an ugly bastard, and thus I tend to avoid it."

Here is another example of suspiciously misplaced excitement, this one also from Truss: "If there is one lesson to be learned from this book, it is that there is never a dull moment in the world of punctuation."

Well, if there is one lesson to be learned from *this* book, it's that you don't have to be a dork in order to use a few dots, squiggles, and dashes correctly. Anyone who would disagree, anyone who would have us believe that punctuation is only for a super-exclusive clique of kooks needs to be told loudly and proudly: Kiss my dash.

Punctuation is simple stuff, with just a few confusing gray areas. These gray areas, of course, are where we make our mistakes and, therefore, where punctuation perfectionists find fodder to intimidate the bejesus out of us. But anyone who knows the difference between "the boys' school" and "the boy's school" need never be intimidated by those more knowledgeable. Anyone who doesn't know the difference can, with surprisingly little effort, attain the same punctuation skill level. Besides apostrophes, commas, hyphens, colons, semicolons, and dashes—which we cover in separate chapters— there are only a handful of punctuation marks to learn.

Brackets. For years, brackets couldn't be transmitted over newswires. That's why people with newspaper backgrounds don't believe in them. That's why someone with a background in newspapers is now telling you that you need not care. I suppose some might argue that brackets are useful for showing parenthetical ideas within other parenthetical ideas: "I told Mr. Panda (whose wife [who found lipstick on his collar] just left him) to grow up." But as you can see by the incredible awkwardness of this sentence, there really isn't much reason to care about brackets.

Periods. A period ends a sentence. It always goes inside of the quotation marks: "Lynne told me I was obnoxious."

Use the period outside of a parenthesis when the stuff inside the parenthesis is not a complete sentence: "These pretzels are making me thirsty (very thirsty)."

But when the stuff in the parenthesis is one or more complete sentences, then periods should show that: "These pretzels are making me thirsty. (That's true partly because they're salty and partly because I'm getting dehydrated worrying the creators of *Seinfeld* will sue me for stealing their line.) I think I'll lay off the pretzels until my iced tea arrives (or my lawyer)."

Periods are usually used with initials—E. B. White—but not with acronyms—CIA.

Parentheses. Here's a too-late bulletin for the mighty creators of punctuation: If you want people to understand the concept behind a punctuation mark, how about giving it a name that doesn't trip people up before they're even out of the gate? The first time I gave any thought to parentheses, I realized I didn't know how to spell the word. Is it "parenthesis" or "parentheses"? Is one of the little crescents, (, a "parenthesis" and the pair of them "parentheses"? Then I realized that I had the same problem with "ellipsis" and "ellipses."

Being the good American that I am, I postponed looking

them up until I absolutely had to (i.e., five minutes ago). Sayeth *Webster's*: "parenthesis: either or both of the curved lines, ( ), used to mark off parenthetical words, etc."

The plural of "parenthesis" is "parentheses."

So you could say this, (, is a "parenthesis" and the set, ( ), are "parentheses." Or you could say that the set, ( ), is a parenthesis and multiple sets are parentheses. Feel free to forget that. I already have.

The important thing (I say) is that you know how to use them, which you already do. Parentheses denote little asides too puny to even be set off by commas. Don't use these marks to set up numbered lists, by the way.

1)
2)
... and so on.

It annoys meanies so much that it's not worth arguing about. Use periods.

1.
2.

Ellipses. Finally looking this up for the first time, I see that, unlike "parenthesis" and "parentheses," the words "ellipsis" and "ellipses" are not interchangeable. One set of three dots is an ellipsis, multiple sets of dots are ellipses, each individual dot is an ellipsis point.

Ellipses denote either omitted information, often within a quote, or a trailing off, often by a heavy drinker. Those of you who are not heavy drinkers might have noticed that sometimes there are four dots in an ellipsis. There's a reason for that. When an ellipsis is standing in for missing words within a single sentence, you only need the three dots. "I did ... have relations with that woman." Notice that there's a space before the first dot and after the last one. (This is what the Associated Press calls treating it as a three-letter word.)

When the ellipsis comes after a complete sentence, that sentence ends with a period first, then come the three dots. "I did not have relations with that woman. . . . Did you know I was a Rhodes scholar?" Notice that there's still a space on each side of the ellipses. So after a complete sentence, it's dot-space-dot-dot-dot-space. Most newspaper and book typefaces these days are inclined to make them look run together, as if there were no space between the first and second dots. But there is.

Question marks. Do you know what a question mark is? If you don't, then you can't understand the last sentence, which means you're no longer reading, which means the only people still reading are ones who don't need question marks defined. Here's the only thing the rest of you need to know: "Guess what" is not a question. It's a command. It gets a period or an exclamation point, but not a question mark.

Exclamation points. Hey, you! Yes, you! If you long for the days when Wally and the Beav would get into all kinds of golly-shucks mischief, then perhaps the exclamation point is for you! A Kurt Cobain fan, on the other hand, wouldn't be caught dead using one.

Chapter 17

Copulative Conjunctions: Hot Stuff for the Truly Desperate

Conjunctions to Know and
Conjunctions That Blow

Apparently, there exist things called copulative conjunctions. I know this because, as I was flipping through my *Chicago Manual of Style* looking for something useful, the word "copulative" leapt off the page at me.

I skimmed the paragraph, driven by the same scholarly mind-set that caused me to look up another "c" word the minute I got my new dictionary. Alas, reality threw a wet blanket onto my prurient fascination with copulative conjunctions. (Though my highbrow inquiry regarding the other "c" word was paid off in spades.)

I quickly concluded that copulative conjunctions are of no real interest. Apparently, the term survives only because grammar snobs cling to it so tightly: It's the most excitement many of them ever get. To us normal people, it's just a name for something we can use just fine even without knowing the term. Still, in the interest of actually providing some information, here's the whole idea behind copulative conjunctions, which are a type of "coordinating conjunction": Copulative conjunctions add on more information to the first part of a sentence. The *Chicago Manual* lists "and," "also," "moreover," and "no less than" as copulative conjunctions and gives the following examples: "One associate received a raise, and the other was promoted," and "The jockey's postrace party was no less exciting than the race itself."

I suppose if I were really hard up for adult entertainment I could read something lurid into these examples of jockeys and raises. But I have a satellite dish, so no need for that.

Chicago tells us that copulative conjunctions are also referred to as "additive conjunctions." Had they called them that in the first place, I never would have looked them up.

Copulative conjunctions, obviously, are just a category of conjunctions—a label. Understanding what the label refers to lends no real insight into conjunctions. Sure, scholars need names and descriptions for things that most of us do without thinking, but that doesn't mean I have to know all these labels in order to use the language correctly.

Here's another reason not to bother learning what the experts say about all the different types of conjunctions: They can't even decide how many different types exist. *The Complete Idiot's Guide to Grammar and Style* says there are only three types. *Chicago* lists seven; Garner mentions only two.

No matter how you count them, conjunctions are pretty simple stuff. Some are even made easy to remember by pop culture icons such as Alicia Silverstone—"as if"—and Jennifer Lopez—"but."

Just as "Schoolhouse Rock" taught me years ago, conjunctions are connectors, "hooking up words and phrases and clauses." They include:

and	since	where
for	although	until
or	though	so that
yet	wherever	whenever
when	so	in order that
before	but	as long as
even though	after	as soon as
unless	because	

Some word pairs that work together also work as conjunctions, such as:

both . . . and	as . . . as	not only . . . but also
neither . . . nor	so . . . as	if . . . then
whether . . . or	either . . . or	where . . . there

All these are called "correlative conjunctions," in case you care, which I recommend you don't, especially since this name isn't smutty.

Some words that are usually adverbs can be used as conjunctions, too. They include "nevertheless," "otherwise," and "consequently."

Assuming that most of these are familiar to you, you already know how to use conjunctions. Understanding copulation is optional.

Chapter 18

R U Uptite?

*Shortcuts in the Digital Age and the
Meanies Who Hate Them*

Some people are horrified by the language shortcuts of the digital age.

"In the world of text messages, ignorance of grammar and punctuation obviously doesn't affect a person's ability to communicate messages such as 'C U later,'" Lynne Truss writes.

Bill Walsh, in a chapter titled "Holding the (Virtual) Fort: Disturbing Trends in the Information Age," writes, "When the shortened form of 'electronic mail' began appearing in print, the question was whether it should be e-mail or E-mail; the lowercase form has clearly prevailed, although using the uppercase would be an acceptable style decision. My faith in human intelligence still hasn't recovered from the development that followed: The predominant spelling among the general public has become 'email,' which is an abomination."

I, too, prefer "e-mail" to "email," but not to an extent that I would trot out words like "abomination" or insult the intelligence of my entire species.

Indeed, it seems that everywhere people are fuming over the audacity of e-mailers, bloggers, and chat-room visitors who shorten the word "are" to the letter "r," the word "see" to the letter "c," and so on.

But with all their freaking and all their wanking, the people who want to stop this trend are failing to see the truly significant language phenomenon taking place right before their eyes. What we are witnessing may be the first time in the history of the language that a communication form has prioritized the writer over the reader. Punctuation, as Truss, Walsh, and the others all so passionately point out, was created with the sole purpose of helping the reader clearly and quickly get the writer's point. Ditto for grammar in general. Ditto for most rules of usage. They help the reader or listener understand. But the information-age shortcuts now shaping the language, which were foreshadowed by advertising shortcuts such as "drive-thru," are designed exclusively for the writer's convenience—at the reader's expense. Because it's time-consuming to scroll through characters on my two-way to spell "see," I put the burden on the recipient to fill in the blanks as I write just "c."

A problem? Well, no, as long as people understand this.

Use these shortcuts whenever you like as long as you're aware of the fact that you're making a demand on the reader. When sending an e-mail to the boss, you probably want to avoid writing "IM2CUTE2BTRU" (unless of course your job title is personal assistant to Justin Timberlake).

Technology presents some other language pitfalls as well, especially when it comes to etiquette. For example, in a chat room, THIS IS YELLING. So sometimes you'll want to give the caps lock key a break.

Also, you might want to take note that sentences such as, "I saw your posting yesterday it was good but I disagreed with some of it I checked the link you referred to it wasn't there," might not be too well received by the reader. In other words, just because punctuation sometimes seems nonexistent on the Internet doesn't mean that it's obsolete.

As to the new vocabulary that accompanies our new technology, you might want to take note of the fact that official spellings change faster than you can Google "Paris Hilton and video."

For example, AP still says to use "Web site" instead of "website," even though many newspapers defy this. Of course, these are the same people who tried to hold back the "online" tide for years by insisting on a hyphen in "on-line." The word "e-mail" continues to take a hyphen, despite Bill Walsh's declaration that the entire human race has crashed its mental hard drive. And "dot-com" has no dot in it.

As for things like "e-solutions," "cybersluts," "phishing," "pharming," and "spamming," well, there's no real way to know what will be a "real" word tomorrow. We all have to struggle to keep up with the changing times. But take comfort in the fact that, in this realm, you're way ahead of the grammar snobs who still cling desperately to a time when spell-checker and grammar-checker didn't threaten their reason for living.

Chapter 19

Literally Schmiterally

By now, you may be experiencing a newfound confidence regarding your language skills. After all, the snobs who've been making you feel stupid all these years have been using nothing more than smoke and mirrors. Many things you thought you were doing wrong you were in fact doing right.

Beware this newfound confidence. It's a slippery slope. In the language world, self-assuredness can curdle into snobbery faster than you can say, "I'm William Safire."

So let's take a little test.

Imagine that one morning you open the *Los Angeles Times* business section and see an article about China's booming auto-parts-manufacturing industry. The article, by James Flanigan, begins with the following sentence:

"In the ever-more-competitive global economy, China is now in the driver's seat—literally."

Do you:

A. Contact your car dealer to find out how and when you can purchase one of these marvels of transportation that's so big that it can fit 1.3 billion people and/or the entire landmass of China into the driver's seat;

B. Write a nasty letter to Flanigan explaining to him that the word "literally" is not synonymous with "figuratively"; or

C. Shrug and turn to the comics page, where the antics of
Cathy and Irving are sure to prove much more
satisfying than picking a fight with a complete stranger
over one word.

If you chose C. congratulations. You're in no danger of becoming a grammar snob (though you may be victim of the
myth that being female is about nothing more than dieting and
shoe shopping). If you chose A. or B. then it's time for a reality
check. Me, I chose D. which was to write a whole column on
the subject.

I'm not the first to take a jab at someone's questionable use
of the word "literally." I distinctly remember years ago a co-
worker laughing out loud recounting the time a television
newscaster said something to the effect of, "The city has been
brought literally to its knees."

At one point, people started using the word "literally" to
mean "sort of " or "kind of " or "almost literally" or "please
note the clever double entendre"—all of which are pretty much
the opposite of "literally." In other words, people use the word
"literally" to mean "figuratively."

The *Chicago Manual of Style* editors think "literally" should
mean "literally":

> "literally." This word means "actually; without exaggera-
> tion." It should not be used oxymoronically in figurative
> senses, as in "they were literally glued to their seats" (un-
> less glue had in fact been applied).

The *Associated Press Stylebook* agrees that "literally" should
mean "literally":

> "Figuratively" means in an analogous sense, but not in the
> exact sense. "He bled them white." Literally means in an

exact sense; do not use it figuratively. Wrong: "He literally bled them white." (Unless the blood was drained from their bodies.)

But beware the temptation to become a grammar snob here. Because the minute you scoff at someone using "literally" to mean "figuratively," a more devoted grammar snob is likely to dig up evidence that you're wrong. A few language experts—ones conspiring to drive the rest of us nuts—defend the use of "literally" as something called an "intensive." According to *Webster's New World College Dictionary*, "literally" is "now often used as an intensive to modify a word or phrase that itself is being used figuratively. 'She literally flew into the room.'"

The dictionary writers cleverly sidestep the danger of putting their own behinds (literally) on the line by adding, "This latter usage is objected to by some."

So, are all these "experts" literally driving you and me to the loony bin? Yes. I call shotgun.

Chapter 20

How to Drop Out of High School in the Ninth Grade and Still Make Big Bucks Telling People How to Use Good Grammar

"That" versus "Which"

How to drop out of high school in the ninth grade and still make big bucks telling others how to use good grammar:

Step 1: Drop out of high school.

Step 2: Party for four or five years.

Step 3: Enroll in college. (Note: This only works at Florida public universities and possibly Yale if your dad went there.)

Step 4: Spend four years absolutely certain that you're the only one there whose brain doesn't contain encyclopedias' worth of accumulated knowledge.

Step 5: Get really mad when friends who learned you

dropped out of high school say, "Pfft! I hardly went. You didn't miss anything."

Step 6: Graduate.

Step 7: Bounce around in bad sales jobs for years before applying for a copy-editing job.

Step 8: Realize the night before your copy-editing test that you don't know anything about copy editing.

Step 9: Cram like you haven't crammed since you realized you were completely unprepared for even the most lackluster state university.

Step 10: Continue to bluff your way through journalism and editing careers until one day you find yourself actually bossing around legendary journalist Robert Scheer.

Step 11: Quit in a huff.

Step 12: Come crawling back two years later to a job schlepping city council stories in Newport Beach.

Step 13: Quit in a huff, but not such a big huff that they don't keep running your grammar column on a freelance basis.

Step 14: Pitch a grammar book.

Step 15: Realize you're completely unprepared to write a book on such an impossibly difficult subject.

Step 16: Cram like you haven't crammed since the last time you had to cram like you'd never crammed before.

Step 17: Notice during the course of your cramming what an inexcusable crock of bull the state of grammar rules are in today; realize that much of your years-long insecurity was for nothing.

Step 18: Point out in your book that the grammar emperors wear no clothes.

Step 19: Spend the rest of your years lounging on the beach at Waikiki.

Going through college with just an eighth-grade education had a lot of obvious drawbacks: no blurry prom night to regret, no popular cheerleaders to resent, no experience with soul-dead teachers determined to snuff the love of learning out of each and every student.

But in one way, missing all these golden moments gave me a powerful edge, especially in the area of language learning. You see, to survive in college, I couldn't afford not to ask stupid questions. Hiding my ignorance was never an option. On the contrary, I showed my ass more than Harvey Keitel. I spent four years doing things like sitting in algebra class asking, "What's an equation?" and sitting in advanced poli-sci classes asking, "How does the electoral college work?"

In other words, I spent four years proving that if you really think there's no such thing as a stupid question, you're just not trying hard enough.

As a result, I became desensitized to humiliation—the very weapon that the grammar snobs use to keep the rest of us living in fear. Sure, just like everybody else I felt stupid that I've never really understood the difference between "that" and "which," but I didn't let this shame stop me from confessing my ignorance repeatedly to colleagues until eventually one told me to look it up. And this shame didn't stop me from calling that same old friend a year later and announcing, in a panic, "I've got a copy-editing test tomorrow and I looked up 'that versus which' and I still need help."

That final humiliation seems to have done the trick, because by the end of the night I got it. By the next day I actually passed this portion of the copy-editing test. And now that I finally get it, I can see where a major source of my confusion came from: merry old England.

Consider the following oh-so-British-sounding sentence:

The college which I attend is better than the college which you attend.

This use of "which" is found in every rung of British English, from the poorest Cockney flower girl all the way up to classic Monty Python sketches. It's not my place to tell users of the King's English how to, well, use the King's English. Perhaps the above sentence would be considered correct over there, even though the *Oxford English Grammar* seems to suggest that this construction is wrong on both sides of the pond. Or perhaps one could argue that *Oxford* leaves just enough gray area to allow the Brits to "which" themselves every which way. Again, not my place to say.

But here's what American users might want to know: "Which" sets off what are called "nonessential" or "nonrestrictive" clauses. (It's the same principle as the one we learned about in chapter 10 regarding how to use commas.) In simpler English, "nonessential" or "nonrestrictive" clauses are simply clauses that can be lifted right out of a sentence without changing its primary point.

The college, which you are attending, admits anyone who can spell her own name.

The main point of the sentence is that the college admits just about anyone. The fact that you are currently attending it is an extra bit of information, an aside. Everything in between the commas can be surgically removed from the sentence without changing the simple point that the college admits flunkies.

These "nonessential" clauses should always be set off with commas: A comma always comes before "which." These clauses can come in the middle of a sentence, as we saw above, or at the end. "It's not a very selective college, which is why you got in."

So while "which" is for nonessential information set off with commas, "that" is for the other stuff—ideas essential to understanding a sentence's main point.

AP says that an "essential" or "restrictive" clause "so restricts the meaning of the word or phrase that its absence would lead to a substantially different interpretation of what the author meant."

Revisiting my example of Brit-speak above, "The college which I attend is better than the college which you attend," try cutting out the stuff introduced by each "which." You end up with, "The college is better than the college." Clearly, the points cut out were integral to the main idea of the sentence, which is why that stuff should have been introduced by "thats" instead of "whiches." "The college that I attend is better than the college that you attend" is the correct way to go.

Of course, you may be asking, why not just say, "The college I attend is better than the college you attend"? Isn't it just as good, if not better, without any "thats" at all?

In short, that's a separate question. When choosing between "which" and "that," apply the nonessential clause rule. When choosing between "that" and no "that," apply your own judgment and know that there's lots of room for personal taste. The most important question is whether omitting "that" could send the reader in the wrong direction.

A sentence like, "The president said the Pledge of Allegiance should remain unchanged," would be a lot better with a "that," as in, "The president said *that* the Pledge of Allegiance should remain unchanged." Without the "that," the first thing the reader sees is, "The president said the Pledge of Allegiance."

Some verbs that, according to the Associated Press, beg for a "that" after them include "advocate," "assert," "contend," "declare," "estimate," "make clear," "point out," "propose," and "state." Words and terms that sometimes beg for a "that" before them include "after," "although," "because," "before," "in addition to," "until," and "while."

If you're not sure, go ahead and use "that." And don't fear the "whiches" anymore, either.

Aloha!

Chapter 21

Well, Well, Aren't You Good?

Adverbs Love Action

Lest it be said that my research for this book was not extremely thorough and far-reaching, I flaunt the following usage example:

Male student: "You sure do make love good."

Female teacher, in bed next to male student: "Well. I make love well."

That fascinating citation serves three purposes at once. First, it demonstrates a common error. Second, it demonstrates how correcting others' errors is so clichéd that animated sitcoms can make jokes about it. Third, it vindicates my decision to spend my late nights watching *Family Guy* instead of reading grammar texts. (That's right, in composing this highly academic work I researched not one but two cartoon shows. You're in good hands.)

Adverb confusion, as demonstrated by the student above, is one of the most common language flubs. Luckily, it's also easy to avoid.

"Good" is an adjective because it modifies nouns, as in, "Mrs. Jones is a good teacher." "Well" is an adverb, and adverbs modify verbs. "She teaches well." Adverbs also modify adjectives, prepositions, and other adverbs.

Many adverbs are easy to spot because they end in "-ly"— "happily," "slowly," "eagerly." But many don't, "well" being a case in point. Oh, and just because "family" ends in "-ly" doesn't mean it's an adverb. It's usually a noun, which is why "a family-oriented comedy" keeps the hyphen.

Be careful with sentences such as, "He keeps his lawn beautiful." This use of an adjective is correct because you're not describing his action of "keeping," you're describing the condition of his lawn, a noun. Consider "He acts well" and "He acts good." In the first, you're describing the verb, to act. In the second, what you're really saying is, "He acts as if he is good." Therefore, "good" is modifying a person and not an action. So both "He acts well" and "He acts good" are correct, depending on which you mean.

Some adverbs take the same form as adjectives and adverbs, "wrong" being an obvious example to anyone who read the introduction to this book. These can be stinkers. For example, we get so used to normal cases such as "quick" having the adverb "quickly" and "slow" having the adverb "slowly" that we're thrown off by things like "fast." For "fast," the adjective and adverb are one and the same. So while teachers who are fast also go fast, those who are slow prefer to go slowly. And, for some students, well, that's good.

Chapter 22

Fodder for Those Mothers

"Irregardless" and Other Slipups
We Nonsnobs Can't Afford

Being an anti-meanie isn't all fun and games. Truth be told, the title actually carries some very grave responsibilities. First and foremost is this: You must now—before God, Jon Stewart, and whoever's sleeping next to you (even if these entities are one and the same)—make a solemn oath. You must swear to never, ever use the word "irregardless."

This is not an imperative to be taken lightly. On the contrary, this is war, people. We must never give the enemy fodder. No one word has more power to discredit our cause. One ill-timed utterance of the word "irregardless" and the snobs have all the reason they need to write you off and dismiss every word you speak thereafter.

They don't care that "irregardless" actually is a word. They don't care how many dictionaries you open up and point to the word "irregardless" sandwiched somewhere between "irrational" and "irregularity." Confronted with this documentation, a seasoned grammar snob will merely snort and point to the definition next to the word—the definition that says that "irregardless" means—that's right—"regardless." Why on earth, they ask, would any educated person use such a lame bastardization of a simple word unless she was trying to sound smarter than she really is? Is it possible that the speaker is jumbling up the nearly synonymous words "regardless" and "irrespective"? the snob might ask in a patronizing tone.

Obviously this is a slip-up we can't afford. Therefore, you must do everything in your power to avert such a strategic catastrophe. But if, despite all your best efforts, this word does accidentally escape your lips in the presence of a predatory grammar snob, your only hope is to "commit to the choice," as they say in acting and improv classes. Don't flinch; don't blink; don't let her see you sweat. Just lean back, suck a little imaginary food from your teeth, and say, "Are you tellin' me that 'irregardless' ain't a word?"

This is the linguistic equivalent of a sucker punch, but it will achieve the desired result. Your opponent will become flabbergasted with rage and say something like, "Oh, heavens!" or, "For goodness' sake!" (It's the closest meanies come to cussing; not even scientists understand why this is.) "I can't believe that someone who actually uses the word 'ain't' is trying to tell me how to use the language!"

To which you reply, naturally, "Are you tellin' me that 'ain't' ain't a word?"

At this point her head will explode, and you'll be the clear victor in a decidedly dirty war. To class things up a bit, you might want to send a note to her family expressing your condolences. In your note, mention that her last wish was that the following appear on her grave marker: "Beloved daughter, sister, and friend, irregardless of anything you might have heard about her."

Now, while such an aggressive defense can save you from

an accident involving "irregardless," there are other traps from which there is no escape. For example, if you pronounce the word "supposedly" with a "b," you're screwed. The dictionary won't help you here. Using your own shortcomings as a weapon by trotting out words like "ain't" will only dig you further into your hole. The word is "suppos-ED-ly," not "suppos-AB-ly." Don't say I didn't warn you.

If you're from the Boston area, you have a unique vulnerability to grammar snobs against which you must shield yourself. People from some parts north, including Beantown, have a tendency to say things like, "I should have went." Call it the Curse of the Participle-ino. But if the team that sold Babe Ruth can overcome its curse, then there's hope for us all. Just remember to say, "I should have gone," whenever you're in the presence of a potential snob. It's just a rule, but one that simply must be observed if we are ever to maintain enough credibility with the meanies necessary to achieve our goal of making them cry.

Chapter 23

I Wish I Were Batgirl

The Subjunctive Mood

As a tot, I was a big fan of the *Batman* TV series. I once wrote a letter to Batman and actually received a reply. It took decades to realize that the reply had been in my mother's handwriting.

My Batmania occurred at such a young age that I really can't remember much of it, but family lore has it that I took this fascination to unhealthy extremes. According to sources close to me, I once dressed up as Batgirl for Halloween. But for me, that holiday didn't end on November 1. No, reportedly I continued to wear the dark tights, cape, and leotard with the Batman-logo sticker on the chest for many weeks after the trick-or-treating had ended. But, in true superhero style, I added my own twist: the cut-off top of a plastic milk jug—the kind with a long, curved spout—worn as a hat.

When I sported this ensemble in public, strangers would ask, "Who are you supposed to be?" No doubt this was a stalling tactic as they tried to remember the name of the state's bureau of child mental health services. I would answer, "I'm Batgirl. But you can call me Batty." Then the stranger would dart in the direction of the nearest pay phone.

Now, if you think that's a tragic tale, consider that that same little girl grew up to find herself sitting among a pile of books trying to figure out why it's correct to say, "I wish I were Batgirl," instead of "I wish I was Batgirl." And if you think nothing can top that tragedy, I'll share with you some of the half-baked answers I got. But before I take you down that long and cruel road, I feel obligated to first provide you with some simple and practical help.

The choice between "was" and "were" usually hinges on a surprising condition: plausibility. If you're talking about something hypothetical, something "contrary to fact," use "were." (That's called the subjunctive.) If you're talking about something that may or may not have really happened—something plausible—use "was," "am," or whatever form of "to be" applies to your subject. (This is called the "indicative," the main mood you use for most speech and writing.)

To better understand the difference between real possibilities and hypothetical possibilities, compare, "If I am batty, I will go to an institution," to "If I were batty, I would go to an institution." The first one is considering something that really could happen. The second is speculation, based solely on conformists' prejudice against us cape-wearing crusaders.

When it comes to the subjunctive, sentences that start with "I wish" or "he/she wishes" are easiest. Because they're pretty much always hypothetical, they always take "were." "I wish I were Batgirl, even though now I only get to dress up as her on the weekends and I have to hide when the mailman comes."

And make sure that any "will" or "would" in a conditional

sentence logically follows. "If I were Batgirl, I would look much better in this leotard." "If I was mentally damaged when I was dropped on my head, I will continue to show symptoms throughout my lifetime."

For practical purposes, that's really all you need to know. In terms of understanding the sinister supervillainy of grammar snobs, there's oh so much more. For one thing, no poor schmo could even get this far on the "was"/"were" choice unless he happens to already know it has something to do with the word "subjunctive."

I'm not sure where and when I first heard the word "subjunctive"—probably French class—but without this crucial bit of information, I'd have been up Guano Creek without a paddle because I would not have known how to look up the subject in a book.

The worst thing about the subjunctive, however, is that while almost every grammar and usage book at your local retailer tells you *when* to use the subjunctive, almost none will tell you *how* to use the subjunctive.

Here's when to use it, courtesy of *Garner's Modern American Usage*: Use the subjunctive for "conditions contrary to fact, suppositions, wishes, demands and commands, suggestions and proposals and statements of necessity."

How? Garner doesn't say. Neither does AP or *Chicago*, or even the super-dreamy boy wonder, Robin.

In French class I distinctly remember verb conjugation tables that showed which word to use in every instance.

> If I were going
> I had gone

I had been going
I would have gone

You get the idea: Little tables that show the exact instances in which to choose "going," "gone," etcetera.

But most English-language reference books for native speakers don't bother to tell you which verb forms actually constitute the subjunctive. They pretend you're already supposed to know, even though they know perfectly well that you don't.

Here's what they're not telling you, which I had to purchase a copy of the pricey *Oxford English Grammar* to discover: The English subjunctive exists in only two forms: past-tense forms of "to be" and present-tense forms of all verbs. The first part of this amounts to something so simple you do already know it: change "was" to "were" in the circumstances listed above. "If I was under mental-health surveillance last week, I'm in big trouble" (indicative), versus, "If I were under mental-health surveillance last week, I would be in big trouble" (subjunctive). The first one is weighing a real possibility; the second one is a supposition, a "condition contrary to fact."

The present tense of the subjunctive, on the other hand, applies to all verbs. But in many cases, it's so archaic as to make you sound like a pirate if you use it. "If I be under mental-health surveillance . . ." Still, there are some cases in which it's actually good to know how to use it.

Take the sentence, "He plans his escape from the Joker's lair." If you wanted to put that as a "statement of necessity," perhaps by prefacing it with, "It's crucial that he . . . ," suddenly you would need the subjunctive of "to plan." But how would you know how to conjugate the verb "to plan" accordingly?

Here's what my scary *Oxford* book told me that no other book would: To form the present subjunctive, you use the "base" form of the verb. Think of the "base" form as the infinitive minus "to."

So how would you conjugate "to plan" in the subjunctive in the example that begins, "It's crucial that he . . ."? Yup, just put in "plan." "It's crucial that he plan his escape from the Joker's lair." Indicative: "he plans"; subjunctive: "he plan."

A couple more examples. Indicative: "she walks"; subjunctive: "she walk." Indicative: "it sits"; subjunctive: "it sit."

Notice that only with "he," "she," and "it" is the subjunctive any different from the indicative. By coincidence, the subjunctive is identical to the indicative in all but the third-person singular, that is, "he," "she," or "it." Therefore, someone who has no idea how to use the subjunctive often gets it right by accident. "I plan the party" (indicative); "It's crucial that I plan the party" (subjunctive).

A lot of archaic uses of the subjunctive live on in old-fashioned idioms. "Be that as it may." "As it were." "Be they friend or foe." Piratey stuff like that.

As if all this weren't (subjunctive) enough to make the rest of us want to bag the subjunctive altogether, language experts are now embroiled in a heated debate over whether you and I should even bother with it. This mood, some say, is archaic to the point of being almost obsolete. Big-time expert H. W. Fowler wrote as far back as the 1920s that the subjunctive was "dying."

Others are hell-bent on hanging on.

You can follow these debates back and forth until you drive yourself batty, or you can rely on one who is already batty to interpret the situation for you. Go ahead and use "were" in hypothetical "if" sentences such as the ones above. Also use "were" with the word "wish." These are the instances in which most experts seem to agree that the subjunctive is not yet archaic. Most other uses of the subjunctive can be written off as stuff for the Riddler.

Chapter 24

Mommy's All Wrong, Daddy's All Wrong

The Truth about "Cans" and "Dones"

I'm going to talk about your mama now. Or, as we're seeing more and more, your momma. Please don't think I'm picking a fight. I'm quite sure that, unlike grammar snobs, the vast majority of you could flatten me with very little effort.

I mean no offense to your mama, your momma, or, if you're an amorous young guy checking out the girls on Miami Beach, your mami. But I feel obliged to point out that something your mother told you all those years was, well, a little off.

Remember how you would say, "Can I be excused?" and she'd correct you, saying it should be "may I"? And remember how you just kind of took this as gospel, revised your request, and left the table with your head hanging low? Well, the *Chicago Manual of Style* contains some bad news for your mama:

"In colloquial English, 'can' also expresses a request for permission (Can I go to the movies?), but this usage is not recommended in formal writing."

By now, however, you shouldn't be surprised that, if your mama knows where to look, she can find some experts to support her side, too.

"Can," say Strunk and White, "means 'am (is, are) able.' Not to be used as a substitute for 'may.'"

But, assuming you ever get the chance and the inclination to resume this decades-old dispute with your mama, you could score the match point by opening pretty much any dictionary.

Webster's New World College Dictionary is on your side: "can. 5. (Informal) am, are, or is permitted to; may."

My old *American Heritage Dictionary* goes even further: "Can 3. used to request or grant permission: 'Can I be excused?'"

Unless your mama wore a tiara to dinner and had six forks at each place setting, the informal "can" was okay.

Why is it then that mamas and daddies (including papas and poppas) have always harped and will continue to harp on the "may"-versus-"can" thing? Those of you thinking that the answer has anything to do with grammar snobbery on your parents' part should wash your brains out with soap. No, the reason that even your own beautiful, noble, and saintly mother harps on this one is not a reflection on her. The reason is simply because some language choices just beg to be nitpicked.

For example, the house I grew up in was anything but a temple of language learning. Yet there was one sentence that always evoked swift correction. Saying "I'm done" was a high crime punishable by sarcasm.

"You're not done. You're not a roast. You're finished."

Despite the bravery I advocated when I was telling you to

pick a fight with your own mama, my courage is nowhere to be found on this one. And the fact that AP, Strunk and White, Bill Walsh, and *Chicago* all completely overlook the "done"-versus-"finished" topic hardly emboldens me. The only authority I've found willing to tackle this one is a force more frightening than all the others combined: Marilyn vos Savant—the woman listed in the *Guinness Book of World Records* as having the world's highest IQ. (I'm not sure how they managed to compare her brainpower with all the poor people in the developing world who've never set foot in a formal classroom, but I suppose that's the magic of standardized testing.)

I should probably keep in perspective that her weekly "Ask Marilyn" column appears in *Parade* magazine instead of the *New Yorker* or the *Atlantic*. But this is a woman who has made a career out of being right, putting mathematicians and the like to shame. Vos Savant scares me. Period.

So, while I could argue either side of the "done"-versus-"finished" debate, I'm not willing to mess with Marilyn. Here's how vos Savant dealt with a reader's question in her column:

"Dear Marilyn: My boss believes that the sentence, 'I'm done,' is grammatically incorrect. He says I should say, 'I'm finished.' I say that you can do something, so you can be 'done.' Who's right?—Annette Wolf, Toledo, Ohio."

Marilyn's answer: "He is. You would say, 'I'm done,' in circumstances such as the following: You are announcing your creation ('I'm done!') or you are declaring yourself adequately cooked ('I'm done')."

What she meant is that the word "do" is never conjugated this way. Its inflections include "I do," "I did," "I am doing," and "I have done." But never is the verb "to do" conjugated with "am" and "done."

After "am," the word "done" is acting as an adjective, not as a form of the verb "do." And as an adjective, "done" has its own distinct definition—one that means, among other things, "created" or "adequately cooked."

If I were to take issue with Marilyn, which God knows I'm not, I might point out that the expression "I'm done with you" is a defensible colloquialism from which one could logically extrapolate, "I'm done."

Also, if I were to take issue with Marilyn, which God knows I'm still not, I might point out that "I'm finished" has a lot of the same problems as "I'm done."

Like "done," "finished" is both a past participle and an adjective. And, like "done," its adjective form has the definitions "completed" and "ended."

So, at first it seems to me that "I am finished" has the exact same problem as "I am done." That is, they both mean not that I have completed something but that I myself am completed.

But there's a catch, one I'm sure Marilyn could pulverize me with were she ever to try. While the adjectives "done" and "finished" have some overlapping definitions, they have some distinct definitions, too. For example, one meaning of "done" is "to be fully cooked." That's a meaning not shared by "finished." But "finished" has a definition that "done" does not— one *Webster's* notes as an "Americanism": "finished . . . 6. done with a task, activity, or concern ('they were finished by noon.')"

Therefore, "I am finished" is okay because it means "I am done with" something. But "I am done" is not okay because the adjective "done" is not defined as "finished with" something.

I'd bet that ninety-nine percent of the people who've nit-picked others for saying, "I am done," had no grasp of the schizophrenic rules behind their own nitpicking. The most likely exceptions being Marilyn and, of course, your own beautiful, wise, and noble mother.

Chapter 25

The Kids Are All Wrong

*"Alright," Dropping "The" Before "the The,"
Where to Put Your "Only," and Other
Lessons from the World of Rock 'n' Roll*

In 1965, four baby-faced young men who called themselves the Who crammed into a studio and recorded the song "The Kids Are Alright." It was a pivotal moment for rock 'n' roll, for the Who themselves, and yes, even for the English language.

The latter is true because, while the word "alright" is as common in the rock world as trouser bulges, it just so happens that it's every bit as fictional. "Alright" wasn't a word when the Rolling Stones recorded "I'm Alright" any more than it was nearly four decades later while the Killers were recording "Everything Will Be Alright." In fact, in the time that the world of popular music cranked out enough "alrights" to generate 3,045 hits in a song title search on TowerRecords.com, the most that the authorities had budged on the matter was *Webster's New World College Dictionary*'s begrudging inclusion of "alright" as a "disputed spelling" of "all right."

So how did this misspelling become the choice of almost every rocker from Joe Cocker to the Beastie Boys? Well, by pinpointing *when* this happened we may be able to infer *why* it happened. You see, Buddy Holly had no spelling problems with his hit "Well All Right." Elvis songs tended to spell it correctly as well. So whatever took place happened sometime in the '60s, which can only mean one thing: drugs.

I picture a Keith Richards type, youthful but already well on the way to permanent brain damage, scribbling an idea for a new song on a gin-soaked cocktail napkin, not even able to spell "baby" and incoherently smushing his "all" into his "right."

The rest is history. In no time flat, the question of how to spell "all right" became secret code to separate the hip artists from the dorks. Today, a songwriter who opts for "alright" is in the company of Bob Marley, Elton John, the Doobie Brothers, Journey, Grand Funk Railroad, and the Beastie Boys. The musical artist who spells it "all right" will find himself in the company of Prescot Pleasanton, the International Submarine Band, and Marlo Thomas and Friends.

In the music world, the only misspelling more popular than "alright" is "gonna." Led Zeppelin, Sublime, Lenny Kravitz, Tom Waits, Jet, AC/DC, U2, Diana Ross and the Supremes, Twisted Sister, and once again the Who are all "gonna" do something.

Personally, I'm a fan of "gonna." Unlike "alright," which suggests the exact same pronunciation as "all right," "gonna" does a better job of representing how people sometimes pronounce "going to."

Say and spell both of these however you want, just know that a grammar snob looking to score some points at your expense will win any fight in which you try to defend "alright" or "gonna." In fact, James Kilpatrick actually wrote a whole column reaming *Vanity Fair* for using "alright" on its cover. The joke was on Kilpatrick, though, because the word appeared in the headline "The Pigs Are Alright"—a play on the Who song that went right over Kilpatrick's head.

Moving on to a mellower musical genre, if anyone ever tells you, "I only have eyes for you," don't be too flattered. What this person may be saying is that everyone else in the world finds you repulsive, or that while you're named on his organ donor card, you can't have his liver or lungs. Let me explain.

Consider the following choices:

> Only I have eyes for you.
> I only have eyes for you.
> I have only eyes for you.
> I have eyes only for you.

The first one, "Only I have eyes for you," means I am the only human being on the planet who wants to look at you. I only. I alone. I'm as good as you'll ever do, baby.

The second one, "I only have eyes for you," can imply the same as the first example. Technically, though, in this case the word "only" applies to the word "have." I only *have* eyes for you. I don't *sell* eyes for you. I don't *pluck out* eyes for you. I don't *cross my eyes* for you. I just *have* them here standing by in case your corneas ever become scorched by gazing upon Keith Richards in the stark light of day.

The third one, "I have only eyes for you," instructs you to stop coveting the speaker's liver and ogling his healthy young heart. His eyes are the sole bequest you can count on. An old man in Brooklyn has dibs on his pancreas. His private parts are currently the property of your sister.

The last one is the correctly worded version of what the more common expression is supposed to mean. "I have eyes only for you" means everybody else grosses me out or, at the very least, disappoints. But you rock my world.

Think these are just silly technicalities that nobody cares about? Think again.

"Misplacing one's 'only' is a crime against syntax," writes Kilpatrick. "Proper placement of 'only' is a virtue to be constantly applauded." By the way, Kilpatrick is a man of words, for whom "constantly" means "constantly." Therefore, he means that you should keep right on applauding even after your hands begin to bleed.

Or perhaps he's just out of his mind with only-ness. That would explain why he has kicked off every New Year for the last two decades with a column on "only."

Either way, you can see why it's wise to avoid giving these guys fodder.

Ironically, snobs, meanies, and language authorities in general become eerily silent on the very music-related language issues I find most troubling. For example, when I was writing music reviews for an L.A. magazine called *Music Connection*, I could swear an editor told me that music groups should be treated as singulars: U2 *is* a good band, not U2 *are* a good band. I accepted this on faith until I ran into some situations in which that rule seems flat-out ridiculous. Would I really write, "The Backstreet Boys *is* good"? Nope. (They're great.)

So where can you find a clear guideline for dealing with this? AP doesn't seem to have one. I tried looking up "band names," "music," "musical groups," "group nouns," "verbs," "verb agreement," "subject-verb agreement," and "Jagger, Mick, advanced linguistics of." I tried all these in *Chicago* as well, plus "association and organization names," "compositions," "nouns:

plural form with singular sense," and a bunch of other dead ends I chased on the long road to bubkes. Strunk and White, who I believe predate electric guitars, were equally useless. So I e-mailed friends in the editing business with the specific question: "Where can I find a written rule on this?"

Most of my friends did what copy editors and clever politicians do, which is answer the question they wish they were asked instead of the question they were actually asked. They all gave me their opinions, but none could cite a source.

Now, a meanie in my shoes would probably apply the first rule of meaniedom: Cover your ineptitude. You can't go around pretending to know everything if you've revealed that you don't know everything, right? That's why they just pick a side and declare it law. Luckily, I have no such incentive to dodge the subject. Instead, I'll put my own neck on the line and offer some guidelines here and now. As you may have already guessed, that guideline is basically, "Trust your ear and your instincts." But I'll do you one better and be a little more specific.

When the band name is plural, make the verb agree accordingly whenever it makes sense. The Beatles are a good band.

When the band name is singular, do the opposite. Mr. Mister is a truly great band.

Modify that according to whether you're talking about the group as a single entity or as multiple individuals. Mr. Mister are rockin' musicians. Again, do that only when it's clearly the best option. These cases are rare. A better way to state the above would be, "The members of Mr. Mister are rockin' musicians," which neatly wraps up the subject-verb agreement issue while at the same time raising serious questions about your taste in music.

If anyone challenges you on these rules, I suggest you quote the Who's Roger Daltrey: "Who the !@#!! are you?"

Another serious rock 'n' roll language conundrum in which grammar authorities are nearly useless has to do with the word "the" in band titles. You might say, "I'm going to buy the Avril Lavigne CD," but you wouldn't say, "I'm going to buy *the the* Who album."

AP, *Chicago*, and Strunk and White clump this musical matter in with all the others. That is, they ignore it. One suspects these books were written by kids whose parents made them play oboe but wouldn't allow them to buy a single Stones record.

I did find a shadow of a clue in one of these books. Under the heading of "Books and Periodicals," the *Chicago Manual* says it's okay to drop extra "the's," "an's," and "a's":

"That dreadful *Old Curiosity Shop* character, Quilp . . .

but

In *The Old Curiosity Shop*, Dickens . . ."

(Way to appeal to the masses, huh? I, for one, can't shut up about Quilp. I'm all, "Quilp this" and "Quilp that," 24/7.)

Anyway, the point is that when the sentence sets up the name, it's sometimes awkward to leave in the "a," the "an," or the "the." I suppose that would be even more true if you were talking about the '80s group the The, perhaps saying something like, "I thought the the The song said it best."

In all my research, the only reference I found to musical groups was in a section of the *Chicago Manual* titled "Institutions and Companies, What to capitalize." It says:

"A 'the' preceding a name, even when part of the official title, is lowercased in running text." For example, "I read it in the *New York Times*."

There, clumped in with a bunch of highbrow examples such as "the Art Institute of Chicago," "the Library of Congress," and "the Cleveland Orchestra," we see the book's sole and piddly acknowledgment of popular music: "the Beach Boys; the Beatles; the Grateful Dead." So I guess it's a safe guideline to lowercase "the" for the Who (that's what *Rolling Stone* magazine does), the Cure, the Captain and Tennille, and even the The.

With all this evidence that grammar snobs are tragically unhip in the area of popular music, you'd think that at least in this realm they'd keep their know-it-allness to themselves. Not so. In fact, Bryan Garner is even comfortable giving orders to one of the most respected and influential rock musicians of all time.

Pointing out some examples of redundant prepositions, Garner writes: "Paul McCartney, in his hit song 'Live and Let Die,' made a similar error: 'But if this ever-changing world in which we live in, makes you give in and cry, just live and let die.' McCartney might have improved the lyrics by writing 'in which we're livin'.'"

One more time, all together now: "Who the !@#!! are you?"

Chapter 26

How to Impress Brad Pitt

"Affect" versus "Effect"

One of the best things about living in Los Angeles is that here you can be pretty much anything you want to be and nobody blinks an eye.

You can walk around with your hair dyed blue. You can be a millionaire hotshot producer who never wears anything but pajamas inside or outside the house. You can wear a midriff top and a Powerpuff Girls belly-button ring despite being 280 pounds and male. Your "be what you wanna be" options are wide open.

There's only one thing that's utterly and absolutely unforgivable to be in L.A., as illustrated by the story below.

A friend of mine was once at a downtown museum with a date when she noticed leaning against a wall none other than Brad Pitt. (Please note that I cannot confirm the accuracy of this story as Brad Pitt can outrun me and has done so dozens of times over the last eight to ten years.) My friend turned to the man she was with and discreetly whispered, "See over there? That's Brad Pitt."

"Oh, honestly!" her date reportedly burst out, rolling his

eyes (apparently, he wasn't the butch type). "You must be the only person in L.A. who's still starstruck."

You see, everyone in L.A.—and I mean everyone—believes he or she has some pretty important ties to Hollywood heavy hitters. They all know someone who knows someone who knows Gary Coleman; or they once delivered a pizza to the home of a star from *Even Stevens*; or they wrote a screenplay that's sure to be the next blockbuster (usually a powerful and life-altering story about an aspiring writer's struggle to write something).

Therefore, the one thing that an Angeleno should not be is affected by celebrity.

Above-it-all Angelenos are a lot like grammar meanies, without the grammar, of course. Let's call them celebrity-sighting snobs or Hollywood hot-air bags. They're so "in the loop" that they're way, way too cool to notice Britney Spears pumping her own gas or Brad Pitt carelessly lounging within stalking distance.

Give me a break. I bet Jennifer Aniston never got over gasping as she looked in her powder room every morning and said, "Oh my God! That's Brad Pitt who left the seat up!" I wouldn't be surprised if she later giggled to all her friends, "Oh my God! Can you believe I'm divorcing Brad Pitt!" It's only human to be affected by celebrity; it's only normal that celebrity should have an effect. This brings us to this chapter's language lesson.

Please memorize the following two sentences.

Affleck appearances affect all Angelenos.

Even encounters with Emilio Estevez have an effect.

Yeah, yeah. I know that was embarrassingly bad. But I

guarantee it'll help you remember the difference between these two words or your money back (disclaimer: all payments to be made in Confederate bonds).

The most important thing to know about "affect" and "effect" is that "affect" is usually a verb and "effect" is usually a noun, as in "special effects," which people in Hollywood care about a lot, and "side effects," which Hollywood types usually don't think about until it's too late.

There are a couple of annoying little exceptions that grammar meanies will happily use against you if you give them the opportunity. Ever hear someone say, "To effect positive change"? Well, that's a rare example of when "effect" is a verb. Specifically, it's a transitive verb, requiring a direct object, and, according to my beat-up copy of the *American Heritage Dictionary*, second college edition, it means to produce a result, to bring into existence, or to bring about something. You can effect a revolution, an improvement, a transaction—lots of things. But usually there are better ways of saying so.

The other definition of "effect" many readers will recall from their stints in the big house. Flash back to that surly guard dropping your wallet, keys, and "novelty toy" pipe into a plastic bag and saying you'll get back your "personal effects" only if Brad Pitt drops the charges. This "effect" is also a noun, one that means property or possessions.

Not to be outdone, "affect" has a noun form, too. It means disposition or mental state, as in, "Always project a flat affect when meeting an A-list celebrity."

These alternate definitions exist only to confuse and annoy. Ninety-nine percent of the time, "affect" is a verb and "effect" is a noun.

So feel free to use the earlier-stated mnemonic device:

Affleck appearances affect (verb, starts with "a") all Angelenos.

Even encounters with Emilio Estevez have an effect (noun, starts with "e").

Just don't tell Brad Pitt that you got that cornball expression from me.

Chapter 27

And You Too Can Begin Sentences with "And," "So," "But," and "Because"

So you're wondering whether you can begin sentences with "and," "so," "but," and "because"? Because you remember some grammar snob telling you it's wrong? And you're dreading a long, painful grammatical analysis of the matter? But, trouper that you are, you opened to this chapter anyway?

Yes, you can begin sentences with "and," "so," "but," and "because."

Because the *Chicago Manual of Style*, *Lapsing into a Comma*, *Garner's Modern American Usage*, and countless other experts all support sometimes starting sentences with conjunctions, you can do so with confidence.

So there.

Chapter 28

Your Boss Is Not Jesus

*Possessives and Words Ending
in "S," "X," and "Z"*

If your bosses' boss is Jesus's boss, for Jesus' sake, whose boss' son's your boss?

Don't answer that. Don't even try to understand that. Lord knows I don't. Just look at the apostrophes and, before giving in to the urge to kick someone, ask yourself not what Jesus would do, not even what Jesus's apostles would do, but: WWJAD—what would Jesus's apostrophes do?

The answer, of course, is that Jesus was lucky enough to speak Aramaic, a language about which I know absolutely nothing and yet can say with one hundred percent certainty that it contained simpler rules for possessives.

The basic rule for making possessives is among the first things grade-schoolers learn about the English language and is one of the simplest concepts to grasp. To make a possessive, add an apostrophe and an "s." Tiffany's bike. Tyler's puppy dog. Teacher's Xanax.

For most plurals, just add the apostrophe and no "s." The girls' locker room, the boys' attitudes.

Child's play. Or so it would seem, until years later when the child who once wrote the simple story about Tiffany, Tyler, and Teacher decides to write a paper about Jesus's teachings or Marx's theories or the Bushes' dynasty. Then this oh-so-simple concept instantly turns out to be a mess so ugly that the *Chicago Manual of Style* actually encourages readers to discard its own advice: "Since feelings on these matters sometimes run high, users of this manual may wish to modify or add to the exceptions" (a footnote thought by many to also appear at the end of the Ten Commandments).

Possessives start to get ugly when you begin dealing with words that end with "s." Words that end with "x" and "z" confuse many people as well. And from here, possessives get even uglier, prompting the authors of style manuals to list dozens of special cases such as "Nouns the Same in Singular and Plural," "Names Like 'Euripides,'" "Nouns Plural in Form, Singular in Meaning," and "Quasi Possessives." The bad news, of course, is that the rules are so complex and arbitrary that the average person would rather become fluent in Jesus's native Aramaic than learn them. But the good news, as we see so often in the world of the grammar snobs, is that the authorities all contradict each other, leaving you the option of often following your own best judgment.

For example, if you're reading a book about the cultural contributions of Charles Dickens, Karl Marx, and Desi Arnaz, you'd see in the book: "Dickens's, Marx's, and Arnaz's contributions." (You'd probably also be listed on some kind of government watch list, right between Michael Moore and the Teletubbies, but that's a different matter.) If you were reading about the same topic in a newspaper, you'd see the name Dickens drop an "s" while the others kept the extra "s": "Dickens', Marx's, and Arnaz's contributions."

But both the book and the newspaper article would use the identical form when writing, "the bass's mouth, the fox's tail, and the buzz's sound." They would all get an apostrophe and an "s."

That's because, while the Associated Press agrees with *Chicago* on some possessive issues, it disagrees on others. The best news in all this is that, despite many people's fear that words ending in "x" and "z" get special treatment, they don't. AP and *Chicago* agree that, whether common noun or proper name, they just get the standard apostrophe plus "s."

AP and *Chicago* also agree about common nouns ending in "s," such as "boss." These also get the standard apostrophe plus "s." But no matter how big your boss's Jesus complex, no matter how certain he is that he's leading the meek to inherit the earth (I'm looking at you, Bill Gates), no matter how many loaves-and-fishes-style accounting "miracles" he employs in the annual company tax return (I'm looking at you, indicted former Enron execs), your boss is not Jesus—well, at least not according to the Associated Press.

The Associated Press parts ways with *Chicago* when it comes to proper names ending in "s." For proper nouns, including Jesus, AP says, use only the apostrophe but no "s" to make them possessive.

This all means that, while *Chicago* thinks your boss deserves the same treatment as Jesus, the AP, and just about everyone but your boss disagree.

In itself that's a minor disagreement—not too problematic for anyone except your boss. But as we've seen over and over, language authorities can't stand to leave a relatively simple thing alone.

For example, the *New York Times Style Guide*, word columnist William Safire reports, has created a special rule for proper names ending in "s" that happen to belong to "ancients."

"Almost all singular words ending in 's' require a second 's' as well as the apostrophe, with the 'almost' allowing exceptions for Jesus, Moses, Achilles and other ancients," Safire writes.

What's an "ancient"? They're not too clear on that point. But I bet you wouldn't get too far arguing, "Well, Bill Gates seems ancient to me."

Chicago and AP don't make this exception for ancients, though *Chicago* has another cruelly arbitrary rule for another unusual circumstance: "The possessive is formed without an additional 's' for a name of two or more syllables that ends in an 'eez' sound. Euripides' tragedies, the Ganges' source, Xerxes' armies." But that's just for proper names ending in this "eez" sound and not plain old nouns ending with this "eez" sound. So if you tend to write a lot of memos or letters mentioning Euripides, Xerxes, and the Ganges, you might want to make a note of that. I, on the other hand, have already forgotten it.

Most experts agree about what happens when a possessive of a singular word that ends with an "s" is followed by a word that begins with an "s": You drop the "s" after the apostrophe: "the boss's daughter" uses the standard rules of possessives, but "the boss' son" is different just because "son" starts with an "s." Another example: "the hostess's podium," but "the hostess' stand." And another: "the witness's testimony," but "the witness' story." The idea is that otherwise you have three "s" sounds lined up in a row, and that would be crazy.

This most often comes into play with "sake": "for goodness' sake," "for Jesus' sake." But remember, "for heaven's sake" still gets the extra "s" because we're only talking about singulars that end in "s," which "heaven" does not. So I suppose atheists can disregard this rule entirely.

That's okay, because there are more possessives rules to sweat. For example, AP and *Chicago* agree that nouns that are plural in form but singular in meaning—such as "politics," "economics," "species," and "the United States"—get only an apostrophe and no extra "s."

But, yea, though you walk through valley of the shadow of deathly difficult possessives, you need fear no evil, says the good book the *Chicago Manual of Style*:

"'An alternative practice.' Those uncomfortable with the rules, exceptions, and options outlined above may prefer the system, formerly more common, of simply omitting the possessive 's' on all words ending in 's'—hence 'Dylan Thomas' poetry,' 'Maria Callas' singing,' and 'that business' main concern."

Hallelujah.

Chapter 29

The Silence of the Linguists

Double Possessives and Possessives with Gerunds

On his website, Verbivore.com, language expert and author Richard Lederer gives us some chilling insight into his childhood that may also serve as important research into the psychological development of grammar fiends.

"I was the kind of child who, almost as soon as he could talk, saw a butterfly and cooed, 'Oh, goody. A butterfly will flutter by,'" Lederer writes. "Even as a high-school student, I knew that Elvis Presley, born three years before me, would become immortal because I saw that 'Elvis Lives' is a two-word anagram." Further, Lederer reports that he started out in college as a pre-med major but soon realized he was reading chemistry texts "for their literary value."

Is Lederer a grammar snob? I don't know. I didn't read any further. Between the Hannibal the Cannibal–style anagrams, the Buffalo Bill–style preoccupation with butterflies, and the desire to work with cadavers, these few sentences were enough to give me nightmares of Lederer eating my liver with some fava beans and a nice Chianti.

Add to that the fact that, at the very website on which

Lederer, author of *The Cunning Linguist*, brags about enjoying plays on words, there's a note that the site itself was "erected May 1, 1996."

So hopefully you can see why I never got far enough to determine whether he's a serial meanie or just a harmless word perv.

That's okay. As much as we might believe that hard-core language enthusiasts are the only ones who hold answers to some of our everyday language questions, the truth is that the "experts" are often as baffled as the rest of us.

For example, a lot of people, myself included, have wondered whether it's correct to say, "A friend of Dick's," or "A friend of Dick." People love to pretend that they know the answer to this, but the truth is that no amount of cooing or fluttering by will reveal a clear answer. The experts simply don't know.

Sure, the first one, "A friend of Dick's," is a redundancy. The "of" means the same thing as the apostrophe and "s." That's why it's labeled a "double possessive." But that doesn't mean it's wrong, say the authors of the *Chicago Manual of Style*:

"The possessive form may be preceded by 'of' where 'one of several' is implied. 'A friend of Dick's' and 'a friend of his' are equally acceptable."

(That's right. I got "Dick" not by getting overly familiar with Richard Lederer but straight out of the *Chicago Manual of Style*. So when I paraphrase this grammar lesson by saying, "A friend of Dick's is a friend of Dick," you can't pin anything on me.)

Sometimes this double possessive is actually better than the alternative because it eliminates confusion. An example from *Garner's Modern American Usage* shows us that "a bone of the dog" sounds more like part of the dog's body than like something he gnaws on and buries in the yard. "A bone of the dog's" sounds more like a soup bone someone happened to give the dog. Of course, opting for a different construction is often the best way to go: "The dog's bone." (Again, not my example.)

Some grammar snobs, however, refuse to accept this, even if you show it to them in print. They will still insist that "a friend of Dick" is correct and "a friend of Dick's" is incorrect. Here's how to settle their hash: Try replacing "Dick" and "Dick's" with pronouns. It becomes immediately clear that the possessive pronoun "his" is better than the non–possessive pronoun "him." That is, "a friend of his," the equivalent of "a friend of Dick's," is clearly better than "a friend of him," which is the equivalent of "a friend of Dick." That's true even though "a friend of his" is clearly a double possessive. Ditto for "a friend of mine," which anyone would prefer to "a friend of me."

Enter the Associated Press, which throws a bizarre little rule into the mix:

"Two conditions must apply for a double possessive—a phrase such as 'a friend of John's'—to occur: 1. The word after 'of' must refer to an animate object, and 2. The word before 'of' must involve only a portion of the animate object's possessions."

I think this is AP's way of trying to explain why "a member of the church" is better than "a member of the church's" and why "the followers of Reverend Moon" is better than "the followers of Reverend Moon's." But did we really need a rule to tell us this?

Moving on to our second possessive issue, consider the following two choices from the *Chicago Manual of Style*:

"We liked Randy's singing," and "We liked Randy singing." (Again, not—repeat not—my examples.)

The first is called a possessive with gerund, the gerund being the verb ending in "-ing." Some people try to argue that only one of these two approaches is correct. But, as you'll see in chapter 40, bona fide, real-life, doctorates-and-all grammarians can't figure this one out. So you're free to use either.

When comparing, "I disapprove of Randy's lying to the police," and "I disapprove of Randy lying to the police," there's a slight difference in emphasis. The first example says, technically, that what you disapproved of was lying. The second says, technically, that you disapproved of Randy. The ear usually takes care of these nuances for us without our having to stop and think about it (or, if you prefer no possessive, without *us* having to stop and think about it).

Moving on to the third and final possessive issue covered in this chapter, consider this sentence I just made up: "Teachers unions fight for workers' compensation."

Have you noticed in your local newspaper the term "teachers union" without the apostrophe required to make it "teachers' union"? Did you wonder whether perhaps the printing press had broken or that you were going insane?

Newspapers in recent years have found a little loophole in the possessives rule. In a term like "teachers union," the word "teachers" can be considered a possessive or it can also be considered an adjective of sorts. (The books call these "genitive" and "attributive" forms.) Newspapers have used this as a blank check to drop the apostrophes in a lot of terms they use regularly. The problem is, they're making up the rules as they go along and not telling us what they are. "Teachers college" is listed in the *AP Stylebook* as having no apostrophe, where as "workers' compensation" has one.

If they can plead that it's all a matter of interpretation, so can you. Or you can go the even easier route laid out in the

Chicago Manual, which is to always keep the apostrophe except in proper names, such as *Publishers Weekly,* and in cases where it's obvious that no possession is implied, such as "a housewares sale."

These written rules are at best self-evident and at worst ridiculous. So it's a good thing we didn't invest too much time reading the works of grammar snobs, word pervs, or cunning linguists to find answers about Dick, Randy, or the bone of the dog.

Chapter 30

I'm Writing This While Naked

The Oh-So-Steamy Predicate Nominative

I'm writing this chapter while naked: completely, utterly, and magnificently naked. To help you form a mental picture, I'll mention that I look a lot like Pamela Anderson—that is, if you're a man. I look a lot like George Clooney if you're a woman. I bear a striking resemblance to Jude Law if you're not sure. And, if you're Rhea Perlman, I'm the spitting image of a young Danny DeVito.

I stripped down to my birthday suit to get into the spirit of the steamy, sexy subject of this chapter: the predicate nominative. Those of you already familiar with the term are, no doubt, already tingling with anticipation. The rest of you—the virgins to the subject, if you will—should prepare for a life-changing experience that will leave you breathless, spent, yet yearning for more.

Ready? Here we go. Have you ever wondered why it is that when you call, for example, my house and ask to speak with the naked sex symbol, I answer, "This is she"? (Or, to keep with the Clooney, Law, and DeVito examples, fill in, "This is he," "This is it," or "Are you lookin' at my butt?" respectively).

Why would I say "she" or "he" instead of "him" or "her"? That is to say, why would I use the subject pronoun instead of the object pronoun?

Before I answer that, let me slip into this claw-foot tub full of hot, steamy water and bountiful bubbles. Aah! Delicious, isn't it?

Now where was I? Oh, yes. With most sentences, the object of the verb should be the object pronoun. If you'll remember from chapter 2, "I," "he," "she," "we," and "they" are subjects and "me," "him," "her," "us," and "them" are objects. If anyone asked you whether you've ever pictured Jude Law naked you would say, "I've pictured him." You wouldn't say, "I pictured he." The reason, as all you eager enthusiasts have already guessed, is the predicate nominative.

Here's how it works. Whenever you have a noun or pronoun, followed by a form of the verb "to be," followed by another noun or pronoun that's basically the same as the first noun or pronoun, that's called the predicate nominative. Isn't that just spine-tingly-ingly? For a little refresher on the verb "to be," it is conjugated "am," "are," "is," and so on, as in, "I 'am' naked," "You 'are' watching," "He 'is' a magnificent specimen," "We 'are' very bad," and so on. That's the verb "to be."

So, to form a predicate nominative, you'd sandwich this sexy verb between twins, if you will. In fact, you might want to use the following little mnemonic device to help you remember: " 'To be' sandwiched between twins."

For example, in the sentence, "That magnificent silhouette is a naked George Clooney," "That silhouette" and "George Clooney" are the twins. They refer to the same thing.

Now, you ask, why would you need to know this very sexy yet seemingly useless piece of information? To which I'd answer: You're as smart as you are sexy. Because, in the above example, knowing the term "predicate nominative" is completely un-necessary. Even easier is to think of them as "reversible sen-tences." "George Clooney is your secret lover." "Your secret lover is George Clooney."

We should pause here because I'm all goose-bumpy. Better turn this little knob marked "hot" and steam things up a bit. There. Much better. Now, back to business. Only when pro-nouns get involved is it even worth knowing the predicate nominative, and that's because of a silly old rule we naughty little grammar vixens like to break as often as we can. The rule is that when the second of the twins is a pronoun instead of a noun, you use the subject pronoun instead of the object. "That glistening, bubble-covered goddess is I."

I know you like to be bad, so I already know what you're thinking: No way are you going to start talking like that. To which I say, I admire how big and strong and bold and rebel-lious you are.

And I'll let you in on a little secret. I taught you this rule just so you can have fun breaking it. You see, uptight, re-pressed meanies who could use a tubful of Clooney themselves will tell you it's naughty to say things like, "The naked girl you saw? Why, that was me!" or "The sexy guy in scrubs is him." Technically, they're right. In formal English, you should end those two sentences in "I" and "he," respectively.

But when it comes to sinfully sidestepping this rule: Every-body's doing it. So do it all you want. I won't tell.

Now, for any and all of you who might accuse me of using sex to sell an otherwise brain-numbingly boring subject such as the predicate nominative, I say shame on you! You deserve a spanking. To receive your punishment, please form two lines, one in front of Pamela Anderson's house, the other in front of George Clooney's.

Chapter 31

I Wish I May, I Wish I Might for Once in My Life Get This One Right

"May" versus "Might," "Different From" versus "Different Than," "Between" versus "Among," and Other Problematic Pairs

Once upon a time I got a letter from a reader of my column pointing out that I had incorrectly used "different than" instead of "different from." I wrote a new column owning up to the mistake and explaining the difference. A few months later, I got a letter from another reader pointing out that I had again incorrectly used "different than" instead of "different from."

Not two months after writing a column on the difference between "may" and "might," I screwed up in an article and used "may" instead of "might."

After a discussion with a co-worker on the difference between "between" and "among," I promptly forgot the difference between "between" and "among."

After years of following what I thought was a clear guideline on the difference between "compared to" and "compared with," I realized I'd been wrong all along.

And though I've repeatedly looked up the difference between "like" and "as," my writing continues to suggest that I have no idea of the difference between "like" and "as."

Some things just don't stick in my brain.

One of three explanations applies. Either 1. I was dropped on my head as a child, or 2. I was dropped on my head as a child, or 3. some things are hard. Sure, I could drive myself nuts trying to figure out which of the above scenarios explains it, painstakingly researching both grammar and family history until the flat spot on my head throbs. But I'd rather just go over these pitfalls one more time, hoping that this time they'll stick for good.

The difference between "may" and "might" is as clear as the difference between "day" and "day."

"'May' expresses what is possible, is factual, or could be factual," *Chicago* tells us. "'Might' suggests something that is uncertain, hypothetical, or contrary to fact."

So obviously, the difference is as clear as the difference between "possible" and "uncertain." That is, not clear at all.

"Sometimes 'may' means the same thing as 'might,' and there's nothing wrong with that," writes Bill Walsh in terms that leave me wondering whether he skipped English class to watch *Seinfeld*. "If there's some potential for confusion, of course, you can use 'might' if you mean 'maybe' and 'may' if you mean 'allowed to.'"

Is the flat spot on your head throbbing, too? Stay with me.

Strunk and White's guide includes no entry for "may" or "might." The *AP Stylebook* doesn't have one, either. The *Oxford English Grammar*, on the other hand, talks about "may" and "might" a lot, dragging the reader into the deep end of the grammar pool with terms like "modal auxiliaries" and even offering a super-practical explanation of "mayn't" (thanks for that, guys). But *Oxford* never explains the difference between the two words "may" and "might."

How can you dodge the criticism I've suffered for not knowing the difference? I'll make it easy. When choosing between "may" and "might," latch on to the word "hypothetical." Or, better yet, latch on to this word I just made up; "might-o-thetical." With any luck, this will help us both remember that "might" is for the purely made-up stuff while "may" is for things that really may have happened. *Chicago's* examples, unlike its explanations, are helpful:

"I may have turned off the stove, but I can't recall doing so." "I might have won the marathon if I had entered."

The latter is indeed might-o-thetical.

"Between" and "among" are much easier. "Between" is for one-on-one relationships: Tom and Roseanne divided the money between themselves. "Among" is for collective relationships: Tom, Roseanne, and Sandra divided the money among themselves. Note that "between" also works when talking about more than two people or things as long as you're referring to one-on-one relationships within the larger group, as in "trade between members of NAFTA." That's because it's presumed that the trades are taking place one-on-one. Mexico is trading with the United States at the same time that other NAFTA countries are making similar trades.

"Amongst," by the way, is a great word for discrediting yourself with both camps at once, at least in American English. Normal people find "amongst" stuffy; grammar snobs call it an "archaism" that dumb people use to sound smart.

For me, the only hard thing about "between" and "among" is caring. Perhaps that's because, years before, I did make the mistake of caring about the difference between "compared to" and "compared with." The former, I'd learned through various sources, was for metaphors only, as in "nothing compares to you." But years later when I looked this up again, I couldn't find a single source to say I hadn't been using it wrong all those years. Here's the real difference between the two. To "compare to" means to look at similarities. To "compare with" means to look at both similarities and differences. "William Safire's prose has been compared to that of a legal brief." In other words, "compared to" means "likened to." That's different from, "I compared the Hyundai with the Hummer and found that they're both excellent automobiles."

In comparison, "different from" and "different than" are very user-unfriendly. If you'd just as soon steer clear of the whole ugly hornet's nest, just stick to "different from." It's defensible in any situation. You can even cite Strunk and White and the *Associated Press Stylebook* as being one hundred percent on your side. "Different from," they say, is always the way to go. But what the authors of these books don't seem to know is that, while "different than" is often wrong, it's not always wrong.

For you masochists who've not yet turned the page, I'll go on. Though the *Associated Press Stylebook* says unrelentingly, " 'different' takes the preposition 'from,' not 'than,' " consider the following sentence: "Grammar snobs have a different brain chemistry from you and I do." Absurd, huh? Only "than" would make sense here: "Grammar snobs have a different brain chemistry than you and I do."

Yes, the difference hinges on that little verb "do." Yes, it has something to do with the tricky and evil word "than." And yes, changing "you and I" to "us" or "we" in the above example makes the whole mess even messier.

The case for "different than" here is a little thing Bill Walsh calls an "indirect comparison." You're not comparing grammar snobs' brain chemistry to you and me. You're comparing their brain chemistry to your and my brain chemistry. But you're omitting the second mention of this chemistry when you say, "They have different brain chemistry than you and I." Of course, it would be even better to say, "They have different brain chemistry from yours and mine," but if you're determined to use "you and I," it's a clear case for "different than."

In that example, there's an implied verb: either "do," as in, ". . . than you and I do," or "have," as in, ". . . than you and I have." Either way, the implied verb is your hint that the sentence isn't weighing brain chemistry against brain chemistry but instead weighing brain chemistry against "you and I." The parallel term has been omitted. The comparison is indirect.

Another case in which "than" is the clear choice happens when you use the adverb "differently." It would be a little off to say, "She danced the macarena differently from he did." For the same reasons laid out above, "than" is the right choice here.

"Like" and "as" operate on a similar principle. In Strunk and White's terms, "like" applies to nouns and pronouns, while "as" applies to phrases and clauses.

Strunk and White sniffed a baby named Chloe for their example—"Chloe smells good, as a baby should"—while Bill Walsh modified the more popularly cited example of a vintage cigarette ad—"Winston tastes good, as a cigarette should." In both those cases, "as" is the way to go (contrary to the original Winston ad).

"Like" would be the right choice when you say, "Chloe smells like a full diaper," or "Winston tastes like a full diaper," which are both much more realistic than the examples Walsh and Strunk and White gave us.

Chapter 32

A Backyard Barbecue in the Back Yard, A Front-Yard Barbecue in the Front Yard

The Magical Moment When Two Words Become One

Once upon a time, two members of the new landowning class decided to put meat to fire. Bob cooked up some T-bones behind his home. He called it a "back-yard barbecue," being careful to follow the rule that says you're supposed to hyphenate when you make up your own compound out of two words. Aloysius cooked in front of his house, calling it a "front-yard barbecue." Bob, his friends, and his family had a lovely time. Aloysius's friends and family spent the whole day avoiding the pleading stares of stray dogs, gaunt orphans, and Anna Nicole Smith.

It soon became clear to everyone in the neighborhood that the back yard was the place to cook outdoors. These "backyard barbecues" got so popular that it became a household term and eventually found its way into the dictionary as a single word, the adjective "backyard." Front-yard barbecues, on the other hand, never really got off the ground, which is why "frontyard" is not a word, according to *Webster's*.

Absurd as this fabrication is, it's better than any grammar snob's explanation of the logic behind the age-old "one word or two words?" conundrum. (It also adheres nicely to the modern journalistic principle that sometimes truth is duller than fiction—or at least harder to research.)

Knowing when to choose between one word, two, or the combo-with-hyphen is a lot like knowing when you're in love: At the time, it seems so right. In hindsight, though, it's clear that your head was probably lodged up your behind. Then, with the wisdom that only comes after years of experience, you finally realize that everybody's head is up his or her respective behind.

For example, right now, in a workshop near you, people in matching shirts are making signs. Perhaps they work for your own city or county, in your city's or county's very own sign shop. Or perhaps they work for a private firm that has a contract with your local government. Either way, you're paying for their work. And either way, they are, at this moment, doing the exact same thing: stamping onto an aluminum sign the words "Meters Enforced Everyday."

Obviously, they're not doing this for their own entertainment. Someone else told them to—perhaps even someone you voted for, who looked in the dictionary, saw that "everyday" was a word, and subsequently ordered it put onto parking signs that will stand in your neighborhood for years to come. Unfortunately, the signs that will stand for decades as monuments to your city council members' spelling ability should read, "Meters Enforced Every Day."

Like "backyard" and a lot of other words that are formed by mushing together two smaller words, "everyday" is an adjective. If your local Target store offers "everyday low prices," it means they offer these prices "every day." "Day" is a noun here. "Every" is the adjective that modifies it. The Frankenstein word "everyday" was given life and breath only because some trailblazing speakers started saying, "Misspellings are becoming, like, an everyday thing, you know?"

Similarly, "back yard" is two words when it's a noun and one word when it's an adjective. So, your backyard barbecue takes place in your back yard, your local discount store's everyday values are available every day, and, in my opinion, the discussion should end there.

But of course, no such luck.

For example, while *Webster's New World College Dictionary* thinks "backyard" is a valid adjective, it doesn't feel the same about "back seat." There's no such word as "backseat."

The bad news is that you had no way of knowing this without looking it up; the good news is that, once you know it, the rules for turning the noun "back seat" into an adjective are clear: You hyphenate. Someone who hollers driving commands from the back seat is a "back-seat driver." Therefore, you could say that someone who hollers driving commands from the passenger seat would be a "passenger-seat driver."

Not annoying or confusing enough, you say? Then consider this: The above applies only if you're using newspaper style. Books have a whole different set of rules.

For the "back yard" business, blame the Associated Press. They're the ones who, in defiance of dictionaries, insist that "back yard" is two words when a noun. For "back seat," blame some rift in the world of the Websters. *Webster's New World*

College Dictionary, which is the official fall-back reference for newspapers, prefers "back seat" as two words. *Merriam-Webster's Collegiate Dictionary*, the bible for book editors, says the noun should be "backseat."

While there's no way of memorizing all the compounds that, over time, have evolved into single-word adjectives, just understanding these general concepts puts you ahead of the average city council member. When you need to be sure and you check the dictionary, be sure to look for the little "adj.," which means it's an adjective, like "everyday" in "everyday values." If the word appears in the dictionary only as an adjective and not as a noun, then its noun form is two words: "every day." If the compound you're looking for is not in the dictionary at all, such as "passenger seat," then it's two words as a noun and hyphenated as a modifier.

Here are a few specific compounds to be especially careful of:

Anyone—Another question of the speaker's meaning. Consider, "Can anyone help me?" compared to, "Is there any one person who will help?" Then ask yourself which one you mean.

Anyplace—*Webster's New World College Dictionary* lists this as an "Americanism," which means they're not too keen on it. *Webster's Collegiate*—surprise, surprise—disagrees.

Anytime—One word that, by the way, is neither a noun nor an adjective. It's an adverb.

Anyway—A good example of how the speaker's meaning can be the deciding factor. "I didn't care about it anyway" is the correct use of the adverb. But when you're asking, "Is there any way that you can help me?" your noun—the thing you're talking about—is a "way." You could have as easily asked, "Is there some way that you can help me," or "Is there a way that you can help me?"

A while/Awhile—As a noun, it's two words; as an adverb, it's one. "It took quite a while for me to figure this out, so stay awhile and I'll explain it."

Healthcare—Though for years this wasn't a word, now many agree it is both a noun and an adjective. For this one, you must choose a camp. Be aware that the winds are blowing toward one word.

Lineup/Line up—As a noun it's one word; as a verb it's two. "I line up the players to announce who will make the lineup." But *Webster's* does not contain this word as an adjective. So if you wanted to make it into an adjective, what would you do? Well, it depends on which one you mean, the noun or the verb. Chances are, most of the time you'd want to do this would be when talking about the noun—"lineup," for example, when talking about a coach's strategy. And because almost any noun can be used as an adjective—the coach's defense strategy, the coach's field strategy, the coach's player strategy—the noun "lineup" can be used this way as well. Examples in which you might want to use the verb "line up" as an adjective are a bit of a stretch. But if you wanted to talk about how your teacher ordered the class members to line up, you would just hyphenate: "The teacher issued her line-up order. (Told you it was a stretch.)

Longtime—The adjective is one word, unlike "long-term," whose adjective form is still hyphenated.

On to/Onto—When "on" is part of a verb, don't make it part of the preposition. "Log on to the Internet," but "Put the book onto the shelf."

Whichever—All those car-warranty explanations in ads are actually right. It's "10 years or 100,000 miles, whichever comes first."

Chapter 33

How to Never, Ever Offend Anyone with Inadvertently Sexist or Racist Language

Joe Everyman meets Margaret Everywoman at a party.

Joe: Nice to meet you, Margaret

Margaret: Nice to meet you, too. Call me Peggy.

Joe: Okay, Peggy.

One week later: John Doe and Joe Everyman are at a party discussing Margaret Everywoman.

John: Have you met Margaret Everywoman?

Joe: Yes, Peggy seems very nice.

John: Peggy?

Joe: Yes, she prefers Peggy. A lot of Margarets do.

John: Damn political correctness! Damn Margarets! You can't even speak nowadays without somebody trying to control the words that come out of your mouth! Think they can tell me I can't call 'em by their own name? How dare they! I'm going to fire off an angry letter to the editor. Peggy my leg!

* * *

So-called political correctness is really just politeness, but it's politeness once removed. If I ask someone I meet at a party not to call me "Junk in the Trunk," he's happy to oblige, no matter how visibly junk-filled my trunk. But if a third party tells the same guy that bottom-heavy women don't like to be called "Junk in the Trunk" (we prefer "Ladies with a Low Center of Gravity"), somehow that makes him feel muzzled, censored, and really, really cranky.

As a result, the anti-political-correctness contingent out-whined the pro-PC types years ago—no small feat, mind you—and have been moaning like harpooned seals ever since. (Yeah, you heard me right: cuddly, furry baby seals with expressive, intelligent eyes.)

So how, in a cultural climate in which there's no clear line between simple courtesy and a violation of constitutional rights, do you know how to choose your words? How can you be sure to never offend anyone with inadvertently sexist or racist language?

That's easy: Just don't speak or write anything ever.

But what if you're not someone lucky enough to be able to avoid all communication with fellow human beings (lucky schmucks)? How do you manage to never, ever offend anyone with inadvertently sexist or racist language?

You don't. It's impossible.

But I have some good news. Though anti-PC thugs and pro-PC hysterics alike can find fodder just about anywhere, they're really just a tiny minority. Reasonable people—that is, most people—can tell when your heart's in the right place. A little sensitivity goes a long way. Unless you write something really ignorant or rude, you don't need to tippy-toe around every word you choose.

The central principle of politeness is simply to put yourself in the other guy's, woman's, hermaphrodite's, or Martian-American's shoes.

For example, my work sometimes requires me to read television scripts, all of which seem to have the same, very telling quirk. The protagonist might be described as, "Mike: A thirty-something with a hip attitude." Other main characters might be, "Karen: A great-looking woman in her twenties," and "Jack: A fortyish card shark." Then, a little later in the script, another character enters: "Raymond, a black guy in his twenties."

Retroactively, we're to assume that all characters are presumed white unless specified otherwise. This is quite understandable to anyone who has a TV. Imagine any of today's top medical or crime dramas with all the white actors switched for black ones and vice versa and you'll see that, on TV, "presumed white" is often a safe assumption. But you've got to admit that it's a little insulting to everyone else.

In a lot of other arenas, we see a "presumed male" dynamic at work. If you don't believe me, ask yourself: When was the last time you caught a fish and said, "She was a fighter"? When was the last time that you were chasing a cockroach and said, "Where did she go?"

Okay, maybe I'm not breaking your heart with how unfair it is that we women aren't more frequently associated with cockroaches and largemouth bass. But this extends to things like doctors, too, as in, "Who's your family doctor and is he good?"

It's human nature to make assumptions based on our own experiences. If you travel in mostly white circles, "a guy" might automatically refer to a white guy, though you might go out of your way to specify another race: "a Hispanic guy." Innocent enough.

But here's the rub: Context is everything. The mass-communicated word is heard in a different, much broader context than the individual cultural experience from which it's spoken or written. Something you say to the Little League team you coach takes on a completely different meaning when it's broadcast on ESPN.

Context is also altered by the speaker. Consider that if a white person is talking about black people, the pronoun to stand in for "black people" is "them." But if a black person is talking about black people, the corresponding pronoun is "us." So when white people complain that there's an unfair double standard governing how people can talk about race, that's because they don't understand the extent to which things like context and speaker change the very meaning of a word—change it to the point where it can actually have opposite meanings: "them" and "us."

I suggest that, instead of leveling our anger at groups of "others," we band together by channeling our white-hot rage toward the only group that truly deserves it: grammar snobs. After all, these are the people who keep pounding the language rules that make this already difficult area flat-out impossible.

Consider the following sentences:

The reader can take this advice or he can ignore it.
The reader can take this advice or she can ignore it.
The reader can take this advice or he or she can ignore it.
The reader can take this advice or they can ignore it.

Which one's right? None of them. They're all disasters. And, short of completely restructuring the sentence, there's no good alternative, either. English doesn't have a neuter pronoun. Choosing the male pronoun is standard but arguably a little sexist. Choosing the female pronoun incurs the wrath of the anti-PC police. Choosing "he or she" gets awkward really,

really fast. Choosing the plural pronoun "they" is just grammatically wrong and there are hordes of grammar snobs eagerly awaiting the opportunity to tell you so.

Basically, you're screwed.

I'd like to predict that, sometime in the next century, "they," "their," and "them" will become acceptable as neuter pronouns, but by then the junk in my trunk will be sagging so low that all I'll care about is finding the ultimate girdle.

While we wait for that glorious day, I suggest you find your own creative mix for dealing with this. Sometimes just recast your sentences. "Readers can take this advice or they can ignore it." Sometimes reach for the obvious "he." Sometimes give a nod to the dissed group by using "she." Sometimes, especially in business correspondence and other formal writing, opt for the most strictly correct "he or she."

Most important, don't let a handful of irate blowhards make you feel like you're damned if you do and damned if you don't. It's not true. Attempts at sensitivity—even fumbled ones—really are appreciated.

If we follow these simple guidelines, perhaps someday someone like me can be judged based on the content of my character and not the contents of my trunk.

Chapter 34

Complete Sentences?
Optional!

Enclosed in this chapter, please find evidence that grammar snobs are great big meanies. For example, here are the opinions of some language experts on the use of the idiom "enclosed please find," all cited in *Garner's Modern American Usage*:

"A more ridiculous use of words, it seems to me, there could not be."—Richard Grant White

"How foolish it is to tell your reader twice exactly where the check is, and then to suggest that he look around to see if he can find it anywhere."—Wallace E. Bartholomew and Floyd Hurlbut

"When you read a letter that sounds as if it were a compendium of pat expressions from some musty old letter book of the goose quill period, do you feel that you are communing with the writer's mind? On the contrary, if you have a discerning mind, you know that you are merely getting a reflex from one who lacks taste and good mental digestion."—H. Cramp

(These grouches later attained notoriety for creating the pro-grammar-snob slogan, "You suck, we rule," under the banner of their own advertising firm, Whitey, Cramp, and Hurlbut.)

With people like this running around, it's no wonder the rest of us are afraid to use our own language. And no wonder half-educated snobs are emboldened to pick on others for things such as incomplete sentences, as a reader of my column once did.

A complete sentence, we all know, contains a subject and a verb. Often it contains an object or other such "constituents." But all a sentence really needs to be considered complete is a subject and a verb. "Cramp jeered." "Hurlbut gibed."

In imperative sentences—that is, commands—the subject is implied. "Leave!" "Sit!" "Be quiet!" and "Find it enclosed" are all complete sentences even though there's no stated subject. That's because when we conjugate verbs in the imperative the subject is implied. That subject is "you." "Leave!" means, "You leave." "Sit" means, technically, "You sit." "Be quiet!" technically means, "You be quiet." We almost never say them that way, but that's what such imperative sentences mean.

Sometimes just one word can be a complete sentence. "Go."

So now that we know what a complete sentence is, does that mean it's a crime to sometimes use an incomplete sentence? Depends on who you're talking to. If you're talking to a control freak of a grammar snob, then, yes, it's a crime to ever use anything but complete sentences. But if you're talking to pretty much every professional writer who's ever put pen to paper, including many of the greatest writers of all time, then it's absolutely okay to use incomplete sentences for effect or as a literary device. Kosher. Copacetic. Not a problem.

Okay?

Okay.

Chapter 35

It's/Its
a Classroom Ditz

*Or How I Learned to Stop Fuming
and Love the Jerkwad*

I had one college professor who was a bona fide jerkwad. It took me a while to realize that he was a bona fide jerkwad on account of the fact that I was a bona fide kiss-up. But eventually I got a clue.

Perhaps it was the dirty word he called a group of guys who walked in late. I'm not comfortable repeating that word here. I suppose all those years of writing for a newspaper made me frightened to type words I gleefully say aloud to friends, to my cats, and to uninvited Jehovah's Witnesses. But I'll tell you that it starts with a "p," rhymes with "wussies," and somehow wasn't a surprising thing to hear in a class led by Professor Jerkwad. In fact, now that I think about it, he used the same word while telling a story of the spin doctors who dreamed up the idea of feminine deodorant spray. You get the idea. It's also a word that, it seems to me, would look nice spray-painted in large letters on the side of Professor Jerkwad's car, but any resemblance between this observation and any real crime committed in the late 1980s is purely coincidental.

Rumor had it that Professor Jerkwad had a history of holding classes in bars and using the school's senior class as harvesting grounds for a long string of wives who never seemed to stay married to him past age twenty-eight. Rumor also had it that a few years later he was canned from his job amid some rather unpleasant allegations, but we journalists can't succumb to rumor and conjecture when nonspecific innuendo is so much more titillating.

What I can confirm is that Professor Jerkwad was consistently surly. He was visibly bitter at the world in general and the knowledge level of the typical college student in particular. He seemed to like a couple of students in the class, but the rest of us were just living reminders of why his Ivy League degree was being wasted in an intellectual black hole of keg-party-goers, sunbathers, and business majors.

But it wasn't until the day I went to his office to get the grade on my final project that I realized what a jerkwad he really was. The project was a thirty-page paper that took me half a jillion years to complete and was cranked out over the course of two whole semesters on a portable electric typewriter. It was the biggest project I had ever undertaken, and I was sure it would kill me. Whiting out the typos alone took more effort than I had exerted my entire freshman year.

So imagine my shock when, several weeks after I turned in my paper, I went to Dr. Jerkwad's office to get my grade and he said, "Paper? What paper? You never gave me your paper."

At the time, it was hard to fathom that a professor would do that deliberately or maliciously. There must have been some mistake—his, mine—I didn't see the point of arguing about it.

"I gave it to you weeks ago. I put it in your hand when you were right here in your office. You told me my grade would be available today."

He shuffled through some papers on his desk.

"No. You never gave me your paper."

I was rattled, but not defeated.

"Oh, well, okay. I kept a copy. I'll make you another."

Like I said, until that moment I was willing to chalk it up to some horrible mistake. But the way his face contorted when I said the word "copy" left no doubt in my mind what had happened to my paper. He had "lost" it on purpose.

"Copy? You have a copy?" Alarm was evident in his voice.

Organization has never been my strong suit. For example, my underwear drawer contains underwear, T-shirts, one flip-flop, and a five-pound bag of flour. So I was never the kind of person organized enough to make and file backup copies of school papers. The only reason I had one of this paper was that the original was so loaded with Wite-Out it looked like a relief map of the Himalayas. The photocopies hid the bumpy white splotches.

So, believe me or don't, just know that I'm convinced that Professor Jerkwad really was such a jerkwad that he'd actually lie about never receiving a student's paper—just for a pathetic little sense of power. And that is why it's painful to admit that one thing Professor Jerkwad did earned my gratitude.

Have you already guessed it has something to do with grammar? Good for you! At least one of us hasn't completely forgotten what we're doing here. Next time I get so far off track, please shove some smelling salts under my nose.

When I finally got back my graded paper, on which I earned a B, I took note of one of Jerkwad's many little handwritten corrections on the page. He had circled the word "it's." Next to it, he wrote, "it's = contraction of 'it' and 'is'; its = possessive."

And that, ladies and gentlemen, is pretty much the sum total of my four years of education in a state school, yours free just for indulging my vengeful little waltz through the past, which I realize probably seemed like about four years.

I was ashamed at the time to have confused "it's" with "its"—a college senior, I figured, should have known that already. But I've since observed that a great many college graduates still don't get it. It's a very common mistake. Sometimes it's clear that such mistakes are just typos. I still flake sometimes and type "it's" when I mean "its." After all, every other possessive under the sun takes an apostrophe, so the autopilot function in my brain sometimes forgets that this is an exception. But sometimes you can tell that a writer truly doesn't understand the rule, especially when she makes the same mistake consistently throughout a document. So remember, unless it's short for the two words "it" and "is," or "it" and "has," do not use an apostrophe. If the word has anything to do with possession—"the dog buried its bone," "the college fired its most obnoxious faculty member"—this is the exception to the rule that you use an apostrophe to show possession.

Thank you, Professor Jerkwad.

Chapter 36

Eight, Nine, 10, 11

How to Write Numbers

Ever notice how a book might write out someone's age as twenty-two while a newspaper article about the same person would say he's 22? Ever wonder why fifty-five has a hyphen but two hundred does not, or why that holds true even when you put them together and get two hundred fifty-five? Ever notice that your local newspaper sometimes refers to grades "nine through 12," but 9-year-olds are always 9 even though their years on the planet add up to nine? Ever wonder why some buildings are located on First Street while others are on 1st Street? Ever see in the same book a sentence that begins with the year seventeen seventy-six and a sentence that contains the year 1776? Ever wonder why the same book will say there were a thousand cats until, a few weeks later, there were 1,284 cats? Ever fantasize about writing vividly threatening letters to every editor in the country?

No? Good. That means that we probably won't be seeing you on *America's Most Wanted* anytime soon. And it probably also means that you have no idea the lengths that language experts have gone to in order to make an easy subject incredibly complicated.

Most of these discrepancies about numbers have nothing

to do with right and wrong. They're just a matter of style. And while the Associated Press, *Chicago*, and other writers of guidelines are conspiring to complicate simplicity itself, all you really need to do is pick an approach and remember to stick with it. If you're writing a cover letter and you spell out the number of employers who have not fired you (three), remember to spell out the number who have (nine).

If you're writing something longer than a short letter, though, you might find that spelling everything out gets a little cumbersome, especially if you've been fired one thousand four hundred sixty-five times. Then perhaps AP's guidelines are for you.

According to AP, you should spell out numbers from zero through nine, and use numerals for everything larger. Ages are the exception; they're always numeric. As in the example of "grades nine through 12" above, this sometimes gets a little awkward. But if you have to draw a line somewhere, 10 is as good a place as any.

Is it really that easy? Of course not. There's another rule. Anytime you start a sentence with a number, spell it out even if it's one that would otherwise be expressed in numerals. "Fifty-five out of 56 employers agree I'm worth keeping around for a month." If you're on board with the AP way, years are an exception. Even at the beginning of a sentence, "1776" is not written out.

Is it really that easy? At this point, I'm going to say yes, with one little addition: Really big numbers sometimes get a mixture of words and numerals, which is why you would surely write "$150 million" without having to be told that big numbers sometimes get a mixture of words and numerals.

Is it really that easy? Uh, um, yes. Really this time. But just for fun, let's take a quick look at how books do it.

Spell out "whole numbers from one through one hundred, round numbers, and any number beginning a sentence," the *Chicago Manual* says. That's why when you have a round number of cats, you'd write it out: "I have one thousand cats." But when it's a big number that's not so round, use numerals: "I have 1,284 cats."

Is that really all there is to it? Well, because you've already been subjected to a thousand cruel rules, I'm going to say yes, just to avoid piling on another 1,284.

Chapter 37

If at First You Don't Irk a Snob, Try and Try Again

"Try To" versus "Try And"

Try and avoid "try and." That's what I usually do. I try and come up with ways to remember to say "try to" instead. I try and try and try, but sometimes I forget and use "try and" in place of "try to." So I try and forgive myself for that.

"Try and" is a subject on which the grammar geeks are right but the grammar snobs are rabid. Reasonable people argue that "try and" is a grammatical mess. Snobs argue that any use of "try and" is a personal affront that gives them license to insult others at will.

As I said, "try and" opponents have a strong case. We know that verb compounds use infinitives, such as "to relax," in contexts like, "try to relax." By putting "and" in place of "to," you no longer have an infinitive verb, so you're no longer constructing a correct sentence. Sure, sometimes "and" comes before a verb in the middle of a sentence—"Grammar snobs whine and moan"—but that's because these are two separate actions. It's a different construction from ones that require infinitives, such as, "I want to go," "I ask to be excused," and "I wait to be called on." You'd never say, "I want and go," "I ask and be excused," or "I wait and be called on," because these are all nonsense.

On the other hand, lots of idioms are nonsense, "throw up" being an example that comes immediately to mind. But this doesn't stop the snobs from going ape spit over "try and."

"It drives me crazy to hear 'try and,'" and "It annoys me almost daily," are two of the many emotionally disproportionate comments that have landed in my in-box.

Style book author Bill Walsh bolsters the cause: "Never, ever use 'try and' instead of 'try to.'"

But just because these people try and appoint themselves president of the English language doesn't mean they can try and ignore the even more venerable authorities who disagree.

Strunk and White say to stick to "try to," but they modify this recommendation with the following disclaimer: "Students of the English language will argue that 'try and' has won through and become an idiom. Indeed it has, and it is relaxed and acceptable."

Garner's Modern American Usage goes even further, defending "try and" as a "casualism" in American English and a "standard idiom" in British English.

Once again we see that the average Joe is getting jerked around by people who try and declare themselves the law of the land in blatant defiance of the last person who declared himself the law of the land.

Here's what you should try and remember. When you're speaking or writing for an audience that might include some language aficionados, try and avoid "try and." But when you're faced with a snob, try and drive him up a wall. The best way I've found to try and drive them nuts is by writing a grammar book that crams twenty-three "try ands" into a single chapter.

Chapter 38

Express Lane of Pain

"Less Than" versus "Fewer Than"

True grammar snobs never use the express lane at the grocery store. And it's not just because their shopping carts are usually overflowing with Midol, Preparation H, and the latest issue of *Resentful Loners Monthly*. No, their tendency to avoid the express lane has more to do with that little sign that reads "10 items or less."

Grammar snobs hate that sign. Oh, how they hate that sign. They hate it so much that in some stores we're actually starting to see the results of their complaining, signs that read "10 items or fewer."

The snobs are right, of course. But that just makes them all the more annoying. And it makes it all the more delicious for us—especially those among us who manage grocery stores—to fantasize about somehow exposing their stupidity.

Fantasize no more. Here's a little trick that will send nine out of ten members of the anti-express-lane Gestapo all the way to the back of the store, to the pharmacy counter, to refill their prescriptions for the kind of happiness that only comes to a grammar snob in capsules or tablets.

Just as we saw with "who"/"whom," most people who claim to know the difference between "less than" and "fewer than" often aren't as smart as they think they are. When a grammar snob tells you that your grocer's sign should read "10 items or fewer," I suggest you answer with the following retort:

"That is truly fascinating, O wise one who enlightens me with knowledge. So tell me, if I have eleven items in my cart and I remove one, do I therefore have one fewer item in my cart?"

Your grammar snob will hesitate—one fleeting moment of common sense—before diving headfirst into self-destruct mode.

"Yes," the snob will say. "That's right. You have one fewer item."

At this point, you're legally entitled to burst into a roaring chorus of "We Are the Champions." Eventually, however, you'll have to explain why, exactly, the grammar snob is wrong.

Luckily, the concept is an easy one. The word "less" applies to singular things: less money, less knowledge, less tact. Even when talking about units of measure, such as when talking about "eight gallons of gas," you should usually use "less" because what you're really talking about is not a number of gallons but an amount of a singular thing: gas.

The word "fewer" applies to plural things: fewer friends, fewer social engagements, fewer prospects for happiness.

So when you're talking about the plural items in your shopping cart, the correct choice is "fewer." But when you're talking about one item, the correct choice is "less," as in, "You have one less item in your cart."

So why, you wonder, do people who pride themselves on linguistic superiority mess up such a simple concept?

It's because they're victims of a very common misunderstanding. They believe, as I did until very, very recently (very recently), that "less" is reserved for quantities, especially volume, and "fewer" refers only to numbers of things.

Like most misperceptions, this one has staying power precisely because it's partly true. For example, it explains why you have "less money" but "fewer dollars." It would explain why you may have "less soup" in your bowl but "fewer cans of soup" in your cabinet. It would explain why there's "less gas" in your tank but "fewer miles" racked up on your odometer. In fact, about ninety-five percent of the time, thinking of things this way works just fine.

But the other five percent of the time, such as in the supermarket checkout lane, this logic falls apart. Because the grammar snobs think "fewer" refers to numbers of things and "less" refers to quantities, they're at a loss to understand that, while, yes, the sign should read "10 items or fewer," taking one item from your cart means you have "one less."

So think of "fewer" as a word that applies to plural things and "less" as a word that applies to singular things. That will give the grammar snobs one less way to mess with you and therefore fewer reasons to live.

Chapter 39

Agree to Dis a Meanie

Subject-Verb Agreement, Conjugating Verbs for "None" and "Neither," and Other Agreement Issues

"Subject-verb disagreement [is] a telltale sign of illiteracy," *Lapsing into a Comma* author Bill Walsh writes.

Labeling as illiterate all people who make this grammar mistake is a telltale sign of jock itch or some other ailment that drives people to extreme testiness.

Presumably, Walsh is talking about mistakes such as President Bush's comment on the importance of Syrian troop withdrawal from Lebanon: "There's no half-measures involved." It was a mistake reporters found so forgivable that they didn't even bother to point out that he should have said, "There *are* no half-measures involved."

But not all agreement issues are so simple that they separate the Walshes from the moronic masses. For example, lots of professional writers have trouble making their verbs agree with words such as "none," "neither," and "everyone."

A lot of people think that "none" always means "not one." Following that logic, they think that "none" should always take a verb conjugated in the singular, "none is," and never the plural, "none are."

Not so.

"None is" and "none are" are both correct depending on what you mean.

"Of all the illnesses common to locker rooms, none is as annoying as jock itch," emphasizes that there's not a single ailment as irritating. "There are a lot of cooties you can pick up in the locker room, and none are any fun," emphasizes that there are a number of microbes you might want to avoid.

Unlike "none," "neither" is always singular. "Neither jock itch nor hemorrhoidal inflammation is an excuse to be rude."

The word "everyone" and its stand-in "everybody" are a case study in language anarchy. For example, everyone knows that "everyone" gets a singular verb—"knows"—as in "he knows," and not the plural verb—"know"—as in "they know." Everyone knows this, don't they? But wait a minute. If "everyone" gets a singular verb, shouldn't it get a singular pronoun? "Everyone knows this, doesn't he or she?"

Well, that's what William Safire would have you do.

" 'Everyone' means 'every one,' " Safire writes in *Fumblerules*. "We match our subject, 'everyone,' with its singular pronoun: 'his' or 'her,' not 'their.' "

The examples he gives make good sense. "Everyone does 'his' thing" sounds much more precise than "everyone does 'their' thing."

But sometimes this is flat-out awkward, so awkward that in British English, *Garner's Modern American Usage* reports, it's now correct to use the singular verb but the plural pronoun: "Everyone picks up their keys at the desk."

There's no clear answer to this one, so here's what I suggest: Opt for a singular pronoun—"Everyone applies his own ointment"—in every case except when that's just too awkward. In those cases, go ahead and use the plural pronoun after carefully weighing the fact that it leaves you vulnerable to a grammar-snob attack. "We should give everyone the ointment they need to get relief."

Collective nouns are less clear. They include "couple," "team," "faculty," "memoirs," "media," "data," and "strata." A lot of people like to hand you ironclad rules on these. "Couple," some try to say, should always take a singular verb. "Media," some say, is the plural of "medium" and therefore should always take a plural verb. These are often the same people who number their silverware and arrange dry goods in the cabinets alphabetically. Don't hate, pity. Anyway, once again we have a situation where your ear is a good guide.

"The couple were married Saturday" sounds better than "The couple was married Saturday," right? Now consider this example, which like the previous is lifted directly from the *AP Stylebook*: "Each couple was asked to give $10." "Was" sounds better than "were," huh?

Here's why: "When used in the sense of two people, the word takes plural verbs and pronouns," AP writes. "In the sense of a single unit, use a singular verb." Just as your ear was telling you all along.

For "media," common sense continues to rule over rules. Yes, "media" is the plural of "medium," but it has in recent years come to have a collective meaning, as a synonym for "the press." So when you're talking about a group of media representatives huddled together, sure, use the plural: "The media are chasing J-Lo down the street."

But, as Walsh points out in *Lapsing into a Comma* without interjecting accusations of illiteracy, try substituting "mediums" for "media" and you'll see that sometimes it just doesn't make sense to think of "media" as plural: "The mediums are biased in favor of whichever political party you happen to oppose" sounds dumb and makes it clear that "media" is sometimes a collective and therefore goes best with a singular verb: "The media is biased in favor of whichever political party you happen to oppose."

So for words that describe multiple people or things, just ask yourself whether your sentence is emphasizing a single entity or multiple individuals.

Making your verbs agree with subjects like "politics," "scissors," "measles," and "news" can be harder. For example, "politics" usually is treated as plural: "His politics are wacky." But sometimes it takes a singular verb, especially when it's being discussed as a science or a profession. "Politics is a difficult topic to research." There's no rule to help us, only the dictionary and our own best judgment.

We know "pants" and "scissors" each refers to a single thing, but we always use the plural noun. "These pants are too tight." "Then these scissors are just the thing to help you out of them."

Another place where you want to be careful about agreement issues comes when choosing between "who" and "that." If you're talking about a human being, use "who." "Walsh is the writer who has been picked on enough in this chapter." Not "Walsh is the writer that . . ."

Of course, grammar snobs disagree even on the subject of agreement. But, in fact, agreement is pretty straightforward stuff that we normal people can usually all agree on.

Chapter 40

The Emperor's New Clause

*Pronouns That Are Objects and Subjects,
"Each Other" versus "One Another," and
More Evidence That the "Experts" Aren't All
They're Cracked Up to Be*

Is it, "I appreciate you taking the time to meet with me," or "I appreciate your taking the time to meet with me"?

What's the difference between "each other" and "one another"?

Is it better to say, "Eat spinach so that you will grow up big and strong," or to leave out the "that" and say simply, "Eat spinach so you will grow up big and strong"?

Which is right: "It is I who is going to beat you at poker," or "It is I who am going to beat you at poker"?

Along those lines, is it correct to say, "It is I she loves," or "It is me she loves"?

How many licks does it take to get to the center of a Tootsie Pop?

How many hours have you wasted worrying that somewhere out there people are looking down on you because you don't know the solutions to the problems above?

The answer to all these questions and more: Nobody knows.

When I say nobody knows I don't mean that the experts bicker over the right way to do these things. These are not cases in which they simply disagree. These are cases in which they truly don't have a clue. If they tell you otherwise, they're bluffing. They would like us to believe that they hold such mystical wisdom, but the truth is they're as clueless as the rest of us.

Consider the case of whether you should say, "I appreciate you taking the time to meet with me," or "I appreciate your taking the time to meet with me."

Columnist James Kilpatrick sums up his research by saying, "Grammarians and commentators have been baffled" by the matter. In chapter 29 I gave you some practical pointers on this one, but I spared you the ugly truth, until now.

Webster's Dictionary of English Usage says experts "cannot parse it, they cannot explain it, they cannot decide whether the possessive is correct or not."

The *Chicago Manual of Style* says, basically, see *The New Fowler's Modern English Usage*.

The New Fowler's contains a long story about how H. W. Fowler got into a nasty scuffle in the 1920s with another grammarian named Otto Jespersen over the choice between "women having the vote" and "women's having the vote." Fowler thought the one without the apostrophe and "s" was "grammatically indefensible." He did not, however, see fit to state this belief in the form of a rule in his book *A Dictionary of Modern English Usage*. So seventy years later, editor R. W. Burchfield is left high and dry as he tries to revise Fowler's original work into *The New Fowler's*. He tells us that Fowler eventually admitted that he had underestimated the extent to which respected writers opted for the nonpossessive form. But that's as far as the old guy budged. Wisely covering his own backside, Burchfield too sidestepped trying to state any "rule." In his book, he gives us a long history of the spat, lots of "current practice" examples of respected writers choosing both options, lots of insight into when each option makes more sense—but no rule.

I say avoid awkward structures when possible. "I appreciated John's going to the store for me" has less-awkward alternatives such as, "I was grateful that John went to the store for me." But in general, do whatever you want without fear that someone will think you're wrong. You can write in a thank-you note for a job interview, "I appreciate your taking the time," or "I appreciate you taking the time," without having to fear the recipient will think you're illiterate. The recipient of your letter won't know the "rule" either. If he's so full of himself that he thinks he has the answer to this one, that's not someone you wanted to work for anyway.

The mechanics of the "each other" versus "one another" question are hardly worth getting into. All you really need to know is that you're welcome to use them interchangeably as your ear dictates. Some authorities say that "each other" works best when you're dealing with only two people—"They gave hickeys to each other"—and that "one another" works best with groups—"Employees of the accounting department all gave hickeys to one another." But at least three different language texts argue that there's no basis for this distinction. Use these terms however you like.

As we've seen, the difference between, "Eat spinach so you'll grow up strong," and "Eat spinach so that you'll grow up strong," is also simply a matter of which one sounds better to you.

Most people would never go around saying either, "It is I who is going to beat you at poker," or "It is I who am going to beat you at poker." But at the same time this is a good example of how grammar is so difficult that it can make you feel either hopelessly stupid or so profoundly disgusted that you'd consider switching to Esperanto, Ebonics, or your own primitive system of grunts and shrieks. I could go into the grammatical fine points of this issue, but I don't know or understand them. So I'll tell you simply that if *Webster's Dictionary of English Usage* can't figure it out, you shouldn't feel bad that you can't either. I'm not saying there's no wrong answer. I'm just saying there's no stupid answer.

The choice between, "It is I she loves," and "It is me she loves," is the type of sentence most of us spend a lifetime dodging out of fear our ignorance will be exposed. We just change the sentence to something like, "I'm the one she loves," or "She loves me," wipe the sweat from our brows, and count our lucky stars that we managed to conceal our stupidity. But our stupidity isn't stupid at all.

In most cases, it's technically correct to say, "It is I," "That must be she," and so on. But this rule is useless when the pronoun after "to be" is at the same time the subject of some other verb. "Shall we say 'it is I she loves' or 'it is me she loves'?" the editors of the *American Heritage Dictionary* ask. "There is no strict rule, but given the natural tendency to use objective forms like 'me' rather than nominatives like 'I' in undecideable cases, use of 'me' is entirely defensible here."

So that's what's going on in the highest rungs of language learning. If experts who know more than you and I could ever hope to know remain perfectly baffled by their own area of expertise, the rest of us aren't doing so badly in comparison.

Chapter 41

Satan's Vocabulary

In my research for this book, I have just unearthed a shocking archaeological discovery, a bone-chilling relic that explains more about our language than perhaps we wanted to know. It's a very old newspaper article and I'll let it speak for itself.

SATAN UNVEILS NEW LANGUAGE "ENGLISH" TO TORMENT HUNDREDS OF MILLIONS OF SOULS WITH "DEVILISHLY IMPOSSIBLE" VOCABULARY

By Bernie Crisp

Underworld Times Staff Writer

HADES—The Prince of Darkness this week unveiled a new language he claims will one day terrorize more than half the planet with vocabulary so illogical and treacherous it amounts to a field of "verbal land mines."

"All who doubt my evil majesty, behold: 'flammable' and 'inflammable' are the same!" Mephistopheles said in a press conference on Thursday. "In this new language, your founder can flounder and your flounder can founder! You can be fazed by a phase or phase out being fazed. You can click with a clique. You can feign a feint until you're so faint that you faint! You can hoard your hoard or even a whole horde! You can rein in your reign in the rain! You can complement a compliment or compliment a complement. This is the suffering I unleash on the world. I am Satan!"

The Dark Lord then went on to explain to reporters the goal of this new mechanism of evil.

"Untold millions will stumble; they will fall. And the only way they will be able to escape their eternal shame is by making a pact with me! I am Satan!"

Beelzebub then disappeared in a loud burst of smoke and flame, leaving press secretary Simon Cowell to field further questions. Much to the media's surprise, Cowell began handing out press kits that contained comprehensive guides to the new language's vocabulary.

"Doesn't it defeat the purpose of creating cryptic language if you hand out a guide to that language?" a reporter from the *Tupelo Star-Pentagram* asked.

"Ah, but you underestimate Lucifer," Cowell said. "For herein lies the true evil genius of his plan. All the information—everything you need—to be completely successful within this system will be readily available and right at your fingertips. That way, when you fail—and you will fail—you'll have no one to blame but yourself."

Cowell also said this philosophy will be the basis of a new economic system called "capitalism," but declined to disclose further details.

A sidebar to the newspaper article contained the complete Devil's Vocabulary, which is reprinted here.

WORDS DESIGNED TO TORMENT AND CONFUSE ALL WHO DO NOT BOW TO ME

By Lucifer S.B.D.D.L.P.o.D. Mephistopheles, Esq.

Abstruse/Obtuse—"Abstruse": something that's difficult to understand. "Obtuse": someone who has difficulty understanding: blunt, dull.

Adverse/Averse/Aver—"Adverse" shall mean unfavorable. "Averse" shall mean reluctant. The subtle similarity of the two shall forever torment all who attempt to wield these words. For those who master their use, I create a third just to confuse. That word shall be "aver," a verb meaning to declare something to be true, to state positively, or to affirm. *I am Satan!*

Allude/Elude/Illude—To "allude" is to make an indirect reference to something. To "elude" is to avoid being caught. To "illude" is a very rare word meaning "to deceive." *I am Satan!*

Alternate/Alternative—"Alternate" will be a verb and an adjective meaning to substitute one thing for another, such as an alternate route, or taking turns. It shall also be a noun describing such a substitute. "Alternative" means a choice between things. Only the *Chicago Manual of Style* will even bother trying to explain the difference, and when they do, they will explain it in words as vague as the ones above. *I am Satan!*

Among/Between—"Among" is best reserved for groups of three or more, whereas "between" usually refers to just two. "Miss Lewinsky thought her words were just between us. But among those listening in were some devious people." *I am Satan*, in cooperation with the contributor of the above example, Linda Tripp.

Appraise/Apprise—"Appraise" is to judge the quality, value, or worth of something. "Apprise" is to inform or notify.

Ascent/Assent—"Ascent" is the act of rising, climbing, or advancing. "Assent" is to agree, go along with, or accept an opinion, proposal, etcetera. (I, Satan, grow weary of saying, "*I am Satan!*" Know ye that I am Satan without me having to repeat, "*I am Satan!*"— Satan.)

Awake/Awaken/Wake/Wake up—Because people will have so much need for a word to describe rising from sleep, I create a word grouping so unnecessarily complicated that *Garner's Modern American Usage* will one day write, "The past-tense and past-participial forms of 'wake' and its various siblings are perhaps the most vexing in the language." The most common, "wake up," will have two forms known by all and a third known to none. "Today I wake up." "Yesterday I woke up." And (the obscure one) "In the past I have waked up." Many will think it's "I have woken up." "Woken" will be a legitimate word, but not used with "up." "Woken" shall be an accepted past participle of "wake," especially in British English. As the queen might say, "On many days I have woken in my palace." As one of her American counterparts might say, "On many days I have waked to another day of being Britney Spears." The most important part of my evil plan, however, stems from having four similar terms to describe the exact same thing. The person who ventures to use any besides the common "wake up" shall find himself in a bog. Those four and their past and participle forms are as follows: wake/woke/waked (or woken); awake/awoke/awaked; awaken/awakened/awakened; and wake up/woke up/waked up.

Baited/Bated—The word "bated" shall be virtually unused except in the common expression "bated breath," which the whole world will naturally assume should be spelled "baited." The whole world will be wrong. *I am Satan*, and even though I led you to believe I would stop saying, "*I am Satan*," I am free to say, "*I am Satan!*" whenever my own evilness so inspires me. *I am Satan!*

Calvary/Cavalry—"Calvary" is the place near Jerusalem where the crucifixion of Jesus took place, an outdoor representation of the crucifixion of Jesus, or any experience involving intense pain or anguish. A "cavalry" is a group of combat troops on horses or riding in armored vehicles. (*This one's too easy even for me—Satan.*)

Cite/Site/Sight—A police officer "cites" you by writing you a ticket. He may do so at the "site" (location) of your crime, which you might have committed in plain "sight." If you try to flee, the officer can shoot you if only he can "set his sights" (of his gun) on you.

Clique/Click—A clique is a small, exclusive club, like all those pretty girls in school who always got to go out with the big-man-on-campus types while we less-slutty girls had to sit home dreaming of the day when we'd get our revenge. "Click" is the sound a phone makes when someone's tapping the line. (Another underworld shout-out to Ms. Tripp for her poignant example. *I am Satan!*)

Compliment/Complement—To "compliment" is to flatter or say something nice. To "complement" is to go well with something else. "Complimentary" can mean flattering and also free of charge. "Complementary" means something goes well with another.

Compose/Comprise—Unlike "compose," "comprise" never goes with the word "of." Further, "compose" and "comprise" function almost as opposites. Language is "composed of" words. Words "comprise" language.

Council/Counsel—A "council" shall be the group of people who wield their cruel power over your town's potholes and stop signs. "Counsel" shall be a verb meaning to give advice and a noun referring to my own advocates, the people who give this advice, lawyers.

Decent/Descent/Dissent—One day, observers will see my work in the field of television programming and proclaim, "TV was decent before its descent into nothing but pundits' mindless dissent."

Deserts/Desserts—There shall be a word called "desserts," which shall refer to certain sweet edible things. There shall be a word called "deserts," which refers to arid lands. Then there shall be a third word that sounds just like the first one, is spelled just like the second one, yet means neither. That word shall be "deserts" and it shall be completely unused except in one well-known figure of speech—"to get one's just deserts." No one except those who make pacts with me will ever grasp that it hails from the word "deserve," as in, "to get what one deserves." To further confuse the entire English-speaking world, restaurant critics, paying their dues to me in hopes of someday becoming film critics, shall make nonstop puns of "just desserts." *I am Satan!*

Disburse/Disperse—Give me money, then get out of here.

Disc/Disk—One day, when the land of my new language has fallen to computers, a compact or video disc inserted into a computer shall be spelled with a "c," as shall the brakes of a car. The word disk with a "k" shall refer to all other disk-shaped objects as well as the floppy disk, which is also inserted into a computer but is not shaped like a disk at all. *I am Satan!*

Discreet/Discrete—The first shall mean "sneaky," the second shall mean "separate."

Drier/Dryer—If you're "drier," you shall be less moist than someone else. If you're a "dryer," you're an appliance.

Drink/Drank/Drunk/Drunken—Today I drink. Yesterday I drank. Many times I have drunk. This always makes me drunk, which is why I'm considered a drunken bum.

Ensure/Insure—Only the evil entities one day to be known as insurance companies shall have the power to insure. For all uses besides this form of legal gambling, the correct word shall be "ensure," which shall mean to guarantee or make certain.

Epic/Epoch—"Epic" means heroic, momentous, or grand. It is also a heroic literary work. An "epoch" is a time period or especially a milestone in time.

Faint/Feint/Feign—"Faint" shall be a verb meaning to lose consciousness and an adjective meaning weak, dizzy, or hard to hear or see. "Feint" shall be a noun or verb meaning to fake out an opponent with a false punch, either literally or figuratively. "Feign" shall be a verb meaning to fake someone out by making up an excuse or making a false show: "I feigned a headache."

Farther/Further—"Farther" shall apply only to distances that can be physically measured, be it by ruler, yardstick, tachometer, or some micro-measuring device. "Further" shall mean to advance something or shall refer to figurative distances. For example, one day a governor of a great state shall further his agenda of trying to change the pronunciation of "California." "Further" shall also mean "more," "additional," "additionally," etcetera, further adding to the confusion with "farther."

Faze/Phase—The first one shall linger only in contexts such as, "That didn't faze me," and "He was unfazed by the news." Thus, it shall be so rare that no one will know it when they hear it and will instead think they're hearing the common word "phase."

Filet/Fillet—The person who takes an interest in the subject shall be told that the first is for beef, the second for fish. She shall scratch her head at first, but later pat her own back with pride as she flaunts her wisdom to others. Then, one day, the reckoning will come. She will need verification. She shall open the *Chicago Manual of Style* and find nothing to confirm her long-held belief. Then, in increasing panic, she shall open the *AP Stylebook*, *Garner's Modern American Usage*, *Lapsing into a Comma*, and the *Oxford English Grammar*—none of which shall contain such entries. In a desperate final move, she shall open a dictionary, which shall tell her that a "fillet" is "a lean, boneless piece of meat" or "a flat, boneless slice cut lengthwise from the side of a fish." She will try to save face by concluding that the single-"l" "filet" must simply be short for the French "filet mignon." But her confidence shall be forever shattered. *I am Satan!*

Flammable/Inflammable—To say something is inflammable is to say it can be set on fire, that is, it is able to be "inflamed." Yet the syllable "in" will be confused with the prefix "in," which means "not." Some will believe "inflammable" means not burnable. Many hellish blazes will result. Then, one day, a false prophet will emerge with a plan to save the earth by creating the word "flammable." Fires will be averted, but the human race will burn with frustration over the fact that these two opposite-sounding words are synonyms. *I am Satan!*

Flaunt/Flout—To "flaunt" shall mean to show off. To "flout" shall mean to blatantly disregard or to treat with contempt.

Flesh out/Flush out—To "flesh out" shall be to figuratively put flesh onto bone, "to flesh out an idea." To "flush out" shall be a way to extract a rabbit from the bushes should you want to remove its flesh from its bones.

Flier/Flyer—Authorities shall go back and forth on this, one day agreeing that, in American English, the correct word is "flier" for both handbills and aviators and that "flyer" should be used only as part of proper names, such as "Radio Flyer."

Forbear/Forebear—No one shall care much what these words mean, yet unlike "filet" and "fillet," every stylebook shall offer instruction on them. "Forbear" shall be a verb meaning to tolerate. "Forebear" shall be a noun meaning ancestor. It can be remembered by picturing one's hairy father on a golf course, a bear yelling, "Fore!" But that device shall be far too silly for anyone to write down. The past tense of "forbear" shall be "forbore," its participle "forborne." "I forbore my forebear, who has forborne others before me." *I am silly Satan!*

Founder/Flounder—The first shall mean to sink. The second shall mean to flop around, as a fish might.

Gibe/Jibe/Jive—This trio shall be an important axis of evil in the English-speaking world, with overlapping confusion so widespread that almost no one will be able to get them straight. And within this mess, people will fail to see the single most useful bit of information: that "jibe" is the correct choice in expressions such as, "His words don't jibe with his actions." They might remember this by making a mnemonic with the "j" and the "b," such as, "James Brown's music doesn't jibe with the standards set by Johann Bach." But they shall get too bogged down in the less-useful "gibe," which also begins with a "j" sound and means to make heckling or mocking remarks. "Jive," which shall find its primary usefulness in films such as *Superfly*, shall mean either to get funky or to tease or mock.

Grisly/Grizzly—The first shall mean gruesome. The second shall refer mostly to bears but possess the arcane history of originating from the fact that brown grizzly bears actually have silver-tipped fur. "Grizzly" shall thus continue to mean "grayish." Everyone shall think that a "grizzled" old man is one who is tough and weathered, though in fact it only means that his hair and/or beard are grayish.

Healthy/Healthful—This shall be a favorite weapon for some, who shall hold that, technically, "healthy" means a person or thing in good health, while "healthful" means something that promotes good health. But even those who stand for this truth will be forced to concede that, as the *Chicago Manual of Style* puts it, " 'healthy' is gradually taking over both senses." Though "a healthy diet" is incorrect, practically everyone will say it this way. *I am Satan!*

Hoard/Horde—"Hoard" shall mean to accumulate or an accumulation, the "a" in "accumulate" reminding people of the "a" in "hoard." A "horde" shall mean a large group of people or a nomadic tribe, the "e" serving as a convenient reminder of "everybody" in the horde. Yet most shall never take note of this simple fact.

Home in/Hone in—The first shall originate from homing pigeons, the second shall not exist at all except in the minds of confused people who became confused by the confusion of others who came before them. To assure their continued confusion, there shall be a word called "hone," which shall mean to sharpen, to yearn, or to grumble. But there shall never be the expression "hone in."

Imply/Infer—Most people will not confuse these two words. That will be true in part because it will be so common for people to say, "What are you implying?" But people proud of themselves for knowing the difference will assume that everyone else has trouble with them. Yet nearly everyone will understand that a speaker or writer "implies" something, that is, suggests something. A reader or listener "infers" something, that is, reads between the lines.

Lead/Led—This choice shall trick the ear of even people who know that the past tense of "lead" is "led." "Today I lead a horse to water." "Yesterday I led a horse to water." However, "lead" shall also be a metal whose name is pronounced just like "led," causing people who know better to write, incorrectly, "Yesterday I lead a horse." *I am Satan!*

Lend/Loan—Experts will disagree and give conflicting and confusing instruction. One, Bill Walsh, will offer the practical advice that, to escape "the word nerds' wrath," use "lend" as a verb and "loan" as a noun. This shall make some tempted to correct others who use "loan" as a verb for lending money and "lend" as a verb for lending anything else. Yet this distinction shall be defended by some as well.

Less than/Under, More than/Over—Let the misperception spread far and wide across the land that "less than" and "more than" refer to quantities and "under" and "over" refer to physical locations. This misperception will thus conclude that it's wrong to say, "He received just under a million votes." Let educated people far and wide fall victim to this misperception, only to one day realize they are supported by none and ridiculed by one. "The charge that 'over' is inferior to 'more than' is a baseless crotchet," Bryan Warner shall write. All who read his words will immediately run to their dictionaries to look up the word "crotchet," thereby completely forgetting the lessons regarding "over" and "under." *I am Satan!*

Libel/Liable—"Libel" shall be a written statement that is both malicious and false and therefore fodder for my minions at the American Bar Association. "Liable" shall mean likely or accountable. "She who writes bad things about me is liable to be sued for libel and will thereby be liable for paying a large cash settlement."

Loath/Loathe—The one without the "e" at the end shall mean reluctant. The one with the "e" shall mean to hate.

Lob/Lop—"Lob" shall mean to throw. "Lop" shall mean to cut off. To illustrate this difference, I sacrifice my only begotten son, John Wayne Bobbitt.

Nauseous/Nauseated—Let my minions Strunk and White record it in their evil book as follows: "The first means 'sickening to contemplate'; the second means 'sick at the stomach.' Do not, therefore, say, 'I feel nauseous,' unless you are sure you have that effect on others." Let all who speak the word "nauseous" thereafter use it in a way considered incorrect by Strunk and White and also by the vast majority of language experts, never realizing that they're saying that they themselves are sickening to others! Yet let them be at the same time led in the opposite direction by a most respected tome, *The New Fowler's Modern English Usage*, third edition. "Any handbook that tells you that 'nauseous' cannot mean 'nauseated' is out of touch with the contemporary language." *I am Satan!*

Normalcy/Normality—One shall be more popular than the other, therefore I rule that the other shall be more respectable. "Normality" is thus preferred until the day when people stop saying "normalcy." At that point, I shall change the rule. To facilitate this confusion, both shall be legal.

Palate/Palette/Pallet—"Palate" shall be the roof of the mouth. I shall remember this through the embarrassingly corny mnemonic, "My pal ate." "Palette" shall mean a board on which an artist smears paint, whose two t's I

shall remember by thinking of "Tiny Toulouse-Lautrec."
A "pallet" shall be a low platform for stacking items in a
warehouse and also a small bed. I shall remember its two
l's with, "Let's lift this pallet."

Peaceable/Peaceful—Like "healthful" and "healthy,"
these two will be so commonly confused as to almost render the rule moot. The first shall be an attitude. The second shall be a circumstance. A nation disinclined to war
shall be peaceable. A serene morning or a violence-free
resolution shall be a "peaceful morning" and a "peaceful
resolution," respectively. Yet nearly every newspaper in
the land shall defy this rule by sometimes writing of
peaceful nations and peaceful people.

Peak/Pique—A "peak" shall mean the top of something.
The verb "to pique" shall mean to arouse or provoke, as
in "to pique one's curiosity."

Pore/Pour—One who reads a book very carefully "pores"
over it. One who dumps a full mug of coffee onto its
pages "pours" onto it.

Premier/Premiere—"Premier," besides its meaning as a
leader of a country, is an adjective meaning first, foremost, or most important: "Satan is the universe's premier
creator of mean-spirited vocabularies." A "premiere" is
the first performance or showing of something—a movie,
a play, a television show. Only the one with the "e" at the
end, "premiere," has a verb form: To premiere is to exhibit something for the first time.

Pretense/Pretext—"Pretense" shall mean to fake or put on a false show. "Pretext" shall mean a lie or deliberate deceit. No person shall ever be one hundred percent confident in his grasp of this vague distinction. *I am Satan!*

Principal/Principle—This pairing shall be no more difficult than any other pair of synonyms. "Principal" shall be a noun meaning a person who heads a school or an adjective meaning first in rank or importance. "Principle" shall mean an ethical standard or a guiding fact, such as a "scientific principle." Yet this pairing shall carry its own, unique evil in that countless pasty, middle-aged people across the country will torment children with the excruciatingly unwitty witticism, "Your principal is your pal."

Rack/Wrack—This pair shall be among my favorite torture devices because the first refers to a torture device. "To rack" is to stretch, as if on the infamous rack. Therefore, to think really hard about something will be to "rack one's brain," meaning "to stretch one's brain." To "wrack" is to destroy, that is, to wreck. As a noun, a "wrack" is also an utter destruction. Some will stray from my meanings to say that the two verbs "wrack" and "rack" can be used almost interchangeably. No one will know whom to believe, and thus these words will wreak havoc on the world.

Raise/Raze—"To raise" shall mean to bring up. "To raze" shall mean to tear down. *I am Satan!*

Reek/Wreak—To wreak havoc shall require a "w." To reek shall be merely to stink.

Rein/Reign—The one with the "g" shall mean to rule or govern, like a king. It could be easily remembered that the "g" is for "govern." Yet no one shall take heed. Most shall confuse the reins of the horse with the power of a governor, not realizing the correct phrase is "to rein in."

Sensual/Sensuous—Let my minions at the *Chicago Manual of Style* put it thusly: "What is 'sensual' involves indulgence of the senses—especially sexual gratification. What is 'sensuous' usually applies to aesthetic enjoyment; only hack writers imbue the word with salacious connotations." Let every writer who finds this description less than clear cower in shame over being a "hack." *I am Satan!*

Slay/Sleigh/Sleight—To "slay" shall be to kill. Its forms shall be: "Today I slay," "Yesterday I slew," "Recently I have slain." Many will print "slayed" instead of "slew," misleading others to do the same. A "sleigh" shall be what Santa drives while he's delivering copies of my thinly veiled tool of evil that shall be known as the Harry Potter books. "Sleight" shall mean cunning or power of deception and shall only be heard in the expression "sleight of hand." Many will assume that it's spelled "slight" of hand because they're pronounced the same.

Troop/Troupe—A "troop" shall be a group of soldiers. A "troupe" shall mean a group of circus actors or other performers. One can remember this with the mnemonic, "U are such a drama queen." Likewise, a "trooper" shall be a police officer. A "trouper" shall be one who handles adversity well. The clear implication of this is to suggest that a member of an acting troupe suffers much more adversity than a cop.

Waver/Waiver—To "waver" shall be to go back and forth. A "waiver" shall be a formal relinquishment of a right. Therefore, there's no "I" in "unwavering."

Wet/Whet—The first shall mean moist. The second shall mean to stimulate, make keen, or sharpen, such as "whetting one's appetite." *I am Satan!*

Chapter 42

You Really Can
Look It Up

So now you know.

You know that choices about where to put commas often are not an exact science and that they leave plenty of room for your own judgment.

You know that "John and I" go to the park, but Sarah goes to the park with "John and me."

You know that language rules are so forgiving that you can actually use the word "literally" to mean "figuratively."

You know why *The Simpsons* is the most word-savvy show on television.

You know that James Kilpatrick, William Safire, Lynne Truss, and a whole bunch of other grammar sticklers could all use a good tickling (at the very least).

You know that, despite the seemingly straight lines of my clothed body, naked I'm the spitting image of Pamela Anderson.

You know how to jack up the next meanie who jumps on you for not using "whom."

You know that all those people who want you to think your use of the language is sorely inadequate have been pulling a fast one all these years.

You know how to be right about most language issues most of the time.

That's all great. But what if you need to do better than that? What about the times when it's imperative that you cover your apostrophe?

Well, you could cruise to your local bookseller in search of help, but beware: The meanies are right there on the shelf, waiting to pounce. In fact, about half the language books you'll find in the stores reveal a strange trend that's a clear sign of snobbery. That is, these books go out of their way to identify their audience very clearly in their title or subtitle. *Lapsing into a Comma*, by Bill Walsh, begins its secondary title with *A Curmudgeon's Guide*. Barry Tarshis segregates potential readers by titling his book *Grammar for Smart People*. Eugene H. Ehrlich takes elitism to new levels with his rudely titled book, *The Highly Selective Dictionary for the Extraordinarily Literate*. William F. Buckley Jr.'s *The Lexicon* carries the audience-specific subtitle *A Cornucopia of Wonderful Words for the Inquisitive Word Lover*. Robert Hartwell Fiske's *The Dictionary of Disagreeable English* has the subtitle *A Curmudgeon's Compendium of Excruciatingly Correct Grammar*.

(I must confess that I had the same goal in mind for this book when I pitched the subtitle *Grammar Served with Lots of Sketches of a Nude Homer Simpson*, but I got shot down. Lawyers! Michael Jackson, however, did offer to cover my legal bills if I included images of Bart.)

Eats, Shoots & Leaves takes the secondary title *The Zero Tolerance Approach to Punctuation*. Truss's subtitle openly beckons the intolerant, setting the tone for the "sticklers unite" message they'll find inside. Dig a little deeper into *Eats, Shoots & Leaves* and it becomes clear that Truss has no desire to reach out to the average Joe. "Don't use commas like a stupid person," she commands. That's well and good for her exclusive clique of so-smart readers, but what about us stupid people? Where can we turn?

Enter the second category of grammar and usage books on the shelves: *The Complete Idiot's Guide, English Grammar for Dummies, Painless Grammar,* one that bills itself as a *Grammarphobe's Guide,* one that specifies it's for the *Grammatically Challenged,* and a host of texts that cozy up to us "morons" by making oh-so-charming mistakes in their own titles. These include *Grammer in Plain English,* which has a red slash through the first "e" and a handwritten "a" above. There's also *A Grammar Book for You and I* with a slash through the "I" and the scribbled words, "Oops, Me!"

Golly, Bubba, I was dadgarmed afraid of these here grammar books but this one here really speaks to me.

The only thing left is to come right out and call a work *The Author of This Book Is Your Superior in Every Way and You're Not Smart Enough to Know He's Talking Down to You.*

So, while the "extraordinarily literate" and the "complete idiots" alike have plenty of titles to choose from, what about everybody in the middle? People who went to college, maybe studied a foreign language for a year or two, and demonstrated a decent aptitude for grasping language issues? Those who just want some practical advice without having to get a PhD in English or to wade through verbose musings on the apostrophe by some long-dead member of the House of Lords?

The reigning grammar snobs have no desire to help the majority of people who would like to use the language with greater confidence but who don't want to dedicate their lives to the stuff. And we are the majority. Think about it. Who among us has not, while composing a Dear John letter, fretted over whether to hyphenate "chronic halitosis"? What red-blooded American guy hasn't found himself at a frat party misusing the word "whom" in a vain attempt to score with a hot English major? Who can honestly say she has not, while composing a sonnet, wondered whether to put a comma between "here I sit" and "broken-hearted"?

Yet we're the ugly masses that language experts would rather ignore. In their world, either you're one of them or you're someone they can look down on and patronize.

So I'm going to let you in on one of the biggest secrets of the language-savvy: In between those books that are alternately patronizing, impossible, and perverse, are books with the word "usage" in their titles: *The New Fowler's Modern English Usage*, *Garner's Modern American Usage*, *Webster's Dictionary of English Usage*, *Wilson Follett's Modern American Usage*, and others. These books are the one secret those grammar fat cats don't want you to know because anyone who has one on his desk can handle almost any language situation. Unlike grammar books, which are laid out in the form of someone else's lesson plan, these "usages"/"usage dictionaries" are written for our convenience—not the writer's. And that means that, with one of these books, you can easily access information about exactly what you want to know.

Say, for example, you want to know about when to use "pore" versus "pour." Just look under "p."

> "pore" (to read intently) is sometimes misspelled "pour" (to make [a liquid] flow downward). . . . This probably appears primarily because the verb "pore" appears less often in print.

How's that for a book that's speaking your language? These books are all structured with the same goal in mind: to put the answer to every language question you might have right at your fingertips.

For example, on the same page as "pore" *Garner's* has an entry on "Pontius Pilate," a primer on the difference between "populace" and "population," and a very thorough discussion of possessives.

Want to know how to spell "vale of tears"? Look under "v." Want to know the current rules on split infinitives? Look under "s." Confused about the difference between "load" and "lode"? Turn to "l." "Fused participles" are under "f." "Danglers" are under "d." And, under "g," there's a whole entry on the term "gilding the lily" (unfortunately, it's not dirty). Grammar concepts, commonly confused words, tricky spellings, style issues, figures of speech, notable names—they're all in there, alphabetized.

Neat, huh? These usage guides aren't perfect—they contain some pretty glaring omissions and some clear cases of grammar snobbery. But having one on your desk can make the difference between being language-savvy and living in fear that you're speaking and writing wrong. In other words, your days of cowering before the grammar snobs are over.

So now, as you go forth into the world, remember that your newfound language powers are to be used only for good—never to humiliate the weak but only to fight back against those who do. Your wisdom is for clubbing the curmudgeons and sticking it to the sticklers. Because, once stripped of their power to instill fear in others, grammar snobs are no longer great big meanies—just great big weenies.

Acknowledgments

Every time I watch an awards show, I'm always disappointed that the thank-yous are serious. Never will I have the pleasure of hearing Judi Dench stand before millions of people and say, "I'd like to thank the Prince of Darkness." Never will the world experience the thrill of hearing Sidney Poitier thank all his "eastside homie and gangstas, yo."

Now I know why.

Despite my unrelenting urge to make a joke out of everything, I'm forced to acknowledge that thank-yous are serious business. For example, my agent, Laurie Abkemeier, went above and beyond the call of duty, helping to make this a much better book than it was the first time she laid eyes on it. Thank you, Laurie.

Penguin editor David Cashion gave this little book and me what amounts to our big break—and he did it based on a book proposal that included bathroom humor. His talent and insight improved the book immensely. Thank you, David. All the editors and copy editors at Penguin who worked on this book deserve credit and thanks for saving me from what would most certainly have been some truly embarrassing mistakes. Thank you, people whose names I don't know and who for that reason probably never get the thanks they deserve.

Then there are Tony Dodero and S. J. Cahn, the *Times Community News* editors who didn't scrutinize my credentials too closely when I asked them if I could write a grammar column. Thank you, Tony and S. J.

Then there are all the friends and loved ones whose cheers and encouragement stayed in my head like background music the entire time I was writing this book. They include Stephanie Diani, Jessica Garrison, Donna Stallings, Jeannie Wallace, Bill Mikulak, Kimberly Dickens, Elizabeth Reday, Nancy McCabe, Mallory King, Pat and Ed Averi, and my sisters Diane Cribb and Jennifer Savage. My sister Melanie Sorli was a little farther away, but never far from my mind.

Then there's Dr. Marisa di Pietro, whose profound influence can't be put into words.

Then there's the Starbucks in Studio City, where the electricity I used for my laptop and the water I used in the bathroom surely cost the management more than I spent on coffee.

Then there's Donald Basse, who proves that some grammar sticklers can be both endearing and infectious in their love of the language. Thank you, Don. (Bet you didn't expect to see your name here, huh?) Then there's Deanna George, who taught me some stuff about Angelenos, and Heather "I'm No Grammarian" Hodson, who taught me the word "grammarian."

Last but most, there's Ted Averi, whose loving support and encouragement are rivaled only by his superb editor's instincts and willingness to tell me what I need to hear instead of just what I want to hear. Thank you, Ted.

Thank you, everybody.

Sources

American Heritage Dictionary. 2nd college ed. Boston: Houghton Mifflin, 1985.

Associated Press Stylebook. New York: Basic Books, 2004.

Brown, Dan. *The Da Vinci Code*. New York: Doubleday, 2003.

Buckley, William F. *The Lexicon: A Cornucopia of Wonderful Words for the Inquisitive Word Lover*. New York: Harvest, 1998.

Burchfield, R. W. *The New Fowler's Modern English Usage*. Revised 3rd ed. New York: Oxford University Press, 1998.

Chicago Manual of Style. 15th ed. Chicago: University of Chicago Press, 2003.

Diamond, Harriet, and Phyllis Dutwin. *Barron's Grammar in Plain English*, 2nd ed. Hauppauge, N.Y.: Barron's Educational Series, 1997.

Ehrlich, Eugene H. *The Highly Selective Dictionary for the Extraordinarily Literate*. New York: HarperResource, 1997.

Fiske, Robert Hartwell. *The Dictionary of Disagreeable English: A Curmudgeon's Compendium of Excruciatingly Correct Grammar*. Cincinnati: Writers Digest Books, 2004.

Follett, Wilson. *Modern American Usage*. Hill & Wang, 1988.

Fowler, H. W. *A Dictionary of Modern English Usage*. 2nd ed., revised and edited by Sir Ernest Gowers. Oxford, UK: Oxford University Press, 1965.

Garner, Bryan A. *Garner's Modern American Usage*. New York: Oxford University Press, 2003.

Greenbaum, Sidney. *Oxford English Grammar*. New York: Oxford University Press, 1996.

Kilpatrick, James J. *The Writer's Art*. Universal Press Syndicate, uexpress.com, various dates 2001 to 2005.

King, Stephen. *On Writing: A Memoir of the Craft*. New York: Pocket, 2000.

Lederer, Richard. http://www.verbivore.com/

Rozakis, Laurie E. *The Complete Idiot's Guide to Grammar and Style*. Indianapolis: Alpha Books, 2003.

Safire, William. *Coming to Terms*. New York: Doubleday, 1991.

———. *Fumblerules: A Lighthearted Guide to Grammar and Good Usage*. New York: Doubleday, 1990.

———. "On Language." *New York Times Magazine*, various dates 2004 to 2005.

———. *The Right Word in the Right Place at the Right Time*. New York: Simon & Schuster, 2004.

Strunk, William Jr., and E. B. White. *The Elements of Style*. 4th ed. Boston: Allyn and Bacon, 2000.

Tarshis, Barry. *Grammar for Smart People*. New York: Pocket, 1992.

Truss, Lynne. *Eats, Shoots & Leaves: The Zero Tolerance Approach to Punctuation*. New York: Gotham, 2003.

Vos Savant, Marilyn. "Ask Marilyn." *Parade*, April 10, 2005.

Wallraff, Barbara. "Word Court." *Atlantic*, vol. 295, no. 5 (June 2005).

Walsh, Bill. *The Elephants of Style: A Trunkload of Tips on the Big Issues and Gray Areas of Contemporary American English*. New York: McGraw-Hill, 2004.

————. *Lapsing into a Comma: A Curmudgeon's Guide to the Many Things That Can Go Wrong in Print—and How to Avoid Them.* Chicago: Contemporary Books, 2000.

Webster's New World College Dictionary. 4th ed. Cleveland: Webster's New World, 2001.

FOR THE BEST IN P THE

In every corner of the world, on every subject under the sun, Penguin represents quality and variety—the very best in publishing today.

For complete information about books available from Penguin—including Penguin Classics, Penguin Compass, and Puffins—and how to order them, write to us at the appropriate address below. Please note that for copyright reasons the selection of books varies from country to country.

In the United States: Please write to *Penguin Group (USA), P.O. Box 12289 Dept. B, Newark, New Jersey 07101-5289* or call 1-800-788-6262.

In the United Kingdom: Please write to *Dept. EP, Penguin Books Ltd, Bath Road, Harmondsworth, West Drayton, Middlesex UB7 0DA.*

In Canada: Please write to *Penguin Books Canada Ltd, 90 Eglinton Avenue East, Suite 700, Toronto, Ontario M4P 2Y3.*

In Aust). Box 257,
Ringwood

In New *Bag 102902,*
North Sh

In India *eel Shopping*
Centre, P

In the N *Postbus 3507,*
NL-1001

In Gern *Metzlerstrasse*
26, 60594 *Frankfurt am Main.*

In Spain: Please write to *Penguin Books S. A., Bravo Murillo 19, 1° B, 28015 Madrid.*

In Italy: Please write to *Penguin Italia s.r.l., Via Benedetto Croce 2, 20094 Corsico, Milano.*

In France: Please write to *Penguin France, Le Carré Wilson, 62 rue Benjamin Baillaud, 31500 Toulouse.*

In Japan: Please write to *Penguin Books Japan Ltd, Kaneko Building, 2-3-25 Koraku, Bunkyo-Ku, Tokyo 112.*

In South Africa: Please write to *Penguin Books South Africa (Pty) Ltd, Private Bag X14, Parkview, 2122 Johannesburg.*